Learn Habits of Highly Effective People and Stoicism for Entrepreneurs

Learn Habit Stacking for Success and a Happy Brain. Boost Self Discipline with the Power of the Stoic Philosophy in Modern Life.

By **Pamela Hughes**

"Learn Habits of Highly Effective People and Stoicism for Entrepreneurs: Learn Habit Stacking for Success and a Happy Brain. Boost Self Discipline with the Power of the Stoic Philosophy in Modern Life."
Written by "By Pamela Hughes".

Learn Habits of Highly Effective People and Stoicism for Entrepreneurs is a set of the books "Learn Habits of Highly Effective People & How to Increase Self Discipline" & "Secrets of Stoicism"

Hope You Enjoy!

Table of Contents

Table of Contents
Learn Habits of Highly Effective People & How to Increase Self Discipline
Introduction
Chapter 1 – Habits

    The Importance of Habits
    Cornerstone Habits
    Understanding the Habits of People
    Habits in the Scholarly World
    Authoritative Habits
    Down to Earth Applications
    How Habits Work
    How Do Habits Work?
    Yummy. (The Reward).
    Upgrading Habits
    Useful for Business
    Habit Disturbance
    Identifying Your Good Habits
    Basic Steps to Develop Good Habits

1. Utilize Perception and Assertions.
2. Settle on the Choice, and After That the Responsibility, to Change.
3. Enroll Support from Family and Companions.
4. Identify the Habit.
5. Find Solid Approaches to Remunerate Yourself.
6. Devise an Arrangement.
7. Find Your Triggers and Deterrents.

    Identifying Your Bad Habits
    Identify the Triggers
    Build up a Substitute Arrangement
    Manage the Triggers

Change the Bigger Example
Get Underpins
Backing and Reward Yourself
Use prompts
Be tenacious and tolerant
Consider getting proficient assistance

Chapter 2 – Habits of Highly Effective People

Empowering People
Help Them Reveal Their Zone of Genius.
Give Your Group the Self-Governance to Do It All Alone.
Be a Supplier.
Approach Them What Their Vision Is for Their Vocation or Employment.
Foresight and Focus
Building Strong Relationships
Faith and Commitment
Love and Romance
Analyze Your Passion Level
Sex

> The Amount Sex Are You Having?
> The No-Sex Marriage
> A Prescription for a Better Sex Life
> Discover Two Bits of Paper and Two Pens.
> Remaining Faithful

Ensure Your Relationship

Chapter 3 – Habit Stacking

What is Habit Stacking?
How to Apply Habit Stacking to Your Life

> Build up the Habit of Following the Routine

Case of a Productivity Habit Stacking Routine
Managing Habit Stacking Disruptions and Challenges

The Benefits of Habit Stacking
What Is Habit-Stacking?

> How Habit-Stacking Works
> My Habit-Stacking in Effect
> Habit-Stacking Success Tips
> Approaches to Habit-Stack Your Morning

Chapter 4 – Self-Discipline

What is Self-Discipline?
An Explanation of Self-Discipline
The Reasons for a Lack of Self-Discipline
What Is Self-Restraint?
Benefits of Self-Discipline

> Self-Restraint Benefits and Importance

How Self-Discipline Can Improve Your Life

> What Is Self-Control?
> The Most Effective Method to Develop Self-Discipline
> The Benefits

Fundamentals of Self-Discipline

> Commitment

Optimization
Breaking Point Your Consumption of Caffeine Sources
Inhale Your Way to Becoming a Superhuman
Ponder Your Way to Self-Optimization
Emotions
Continue Practicing Your Emotional Regulation Skills
Exercises to Improve Your Self-Discipline

1. Scrub Down Every Morning
2. Reflect for 10 Minutes per Day
3. Start Your Day With 100 Push-Ups or a 1-Mile Run
4. Make Your Bed

5. Dispense with Distractions
6. Stop Complaining

Self-control and Willpower – Your Inner Strength
Develop Willpower and Self Discipline

Conclusion
Introduction
Chapter 1: History of Stoicism
Chapter 2: Background of Stoicism
Chapter 3: First Two Topoi

- Logic
- Physics

Chapter 4: The Third Topos (Ethics)
Chapter 5: Apatheia and the Stoic Treatment of Emotions
Chapter 6: Stoicism after the Hellenistic Era
Chapter 7: Contemporary Stoicism
Chapter 8: Stoics Spiritual Exercises
Chapter 9: Stoicism Is Ideal for the Real World
Chapter 10: Manage Your Emotions to Find Inner Peace
Chapter 11: Ways to Manage Anger Using Stoicism
Chapter 12: Understanding How and Why Anger Rises
Chapter 13: Stoic Philosophy and Anger
Chapter 14: Stoicism Reveals Rituals That Will Make You Confident
Chapter 15: Stoic Philosophy Ancient Wisdom in the Modern World
Chapter 16: The Four Cardinal Virtues
Chapter 17: Incorporation of Stoic Philosophy into Everyday Life

How to Practice Stoicism

Chapter 18: Growing Up Stoic (Philosophical Education for Character, Persistence, and Grit)
Conclusion

Learn Habits of Highly Effective People & How to Increase Self Discipline

Boost Your Personal Development by Habit Stacking, Stop Procrastinating, Become More Disciplined, and Improve Focus Today!

By Pamela Hughes

Introduction

Congratulations on purchasing *Learn Habits of Highly Effective People & How to Increase Self Discipline* and thank you for doing so.

The following chapters will discuss the habits of highly successful people and how you can adapt them to be successful yourself.

There are plenty of books on this subject on the market, thanks again for choosing this one! Every effort was made to ensure it is full of as much useful information as possible, please enjoy!

Chapter 1 – Habits

The Importance of Habits

Habits are the foundation of your prosperity – or possibly your ruin. However, notwithstanding the significance of habits, few individuals think a lot about how they work.

Habits are regularly thought of as bad things such as having a betting habit. Yet, there can be great habits, for example, practicing routinely, making considerate remarks, considering research themes and hitting deadlines some time before due dates.

A habit is something we do normally without intentionally pondering it. It is a programmed mental and behavioral movement. Habits make it feasible for us to get things done without spending over the top mental exertion. They make regular daily existence conceivable – for positive or negative reasons.

Numerous individuals attempt to get out from negative behavior patterns. Abstaining from excessive food intake is the most outstanding model: it is an endeavor to bring an end to the habit of eating excessively or eating inappropriate sorts of diets. Numerous smokers and heavy drinkers might want to get out from under their habits, and there are a lot of people who might want to support them.

At that point there are habits that block your own personal achievements. Mental habits are significant as well. For instance, focusing on aggravating musings is a habit that can prompt constant nervousness.

In the late decades, specialists have turned out to be progressively mindful of the significance of habits, and there is a developing group of discoveries, quite a bit of it arranged to promote: organizations might want to strengthen or change your purchasing habits.

Cornerstone Habits

For those looking for high-yield results, day by day working is the cornerstone habit. Working with a plan each day animates imagination, centers thoughts regarding what should be perused, encourages research arranging, and much else. there is

Understanding the Habits of People

Realizing that a few habits are harming, scientists have looked for the way to evolving habits. What they have found is that basic habits never vanish. If you have smoked, the desire to smoke can never be completely killed. What can occur, however, is a change to the daily schedule or behavior. At the point when the commonplace signal happens, you accomplish something else, for example, bite some gum.

AA gives an elective daily practice. Drunkards, as opposed to going to a bar, go to an AA meeting. This gives a substitution routine, accordingly fulfilling the hankering. Be that as it may, AA includes one more key component into the procedure: conviction. To change habits, individuals need to trust it is conceivable. Pundits of AA are incredulous of the profound summons engaged with the 12 stages yet conviction is important to AA's prosperity. Besides, being in a gathering of devotees makes conviction simpler.

Building up another habit dependent on brief times of day by day working, and doing the work before you are prepared and when you are not propelled, conflicts with profound situated convictions about how to be an effective scientist. Research demonstrates the program works, however, information of the examination may not be sufficient to conquer dug inhabits. A portion of the keys to utilizing the program are believing that it will work - and thusly making an effort not to re-think the procedure - and going to the gathering gatherings to strengthen conviction. For a habit to remain changed, individuals must accept change is conceivable. Furthermore, regularly, that conviction just rises with the assistance of a gathering.

This is equal to a youthful musician or a youthful swimmer entering a preparation program. You have to accept that the normal activities and preparing are getting down to business, and to confide in the instructor or mentor. Later on, when habits are entrenched, a talented entertainer can tweak the preparation.

Habits in the Scholarly World

In classes that we instruct, we only here and there talk about habits. The concentration in many classes is substance and abilities, and maybe mentalities. Be that as it may, imagine a scenario in which habits are increasingly significant. Think about what is required to turn into a remarkable musician. Research on master execution demonstrates the key is "conscious practice." This is a kind of work on including extraordinary focus on the errand while consistently endeavoring to improve, under the direction of a gifted instructor. In the long haul, habits of rehearsing the violin will have more effect than the specific things learned in any exercise. A huge number of long periods of training are expected to turn into a world-class entertainer. Building up a habit for day by day purposeful practice is the most significant thing to be educated for the objective of master execution.

It is begging to be proven wrong precisely which habits are most beneficial for common expressions understudies. Maybe it is composing, talking, basic reasoning or building up an inquisitive personality. Pick whatever objective you like – on the grounds that most classes do next to no to cultivate a progressing habit. Most understudies study just what they need to: they don't build up a learning habit. Most understudies chip away at assignments just as appraisal due dates approach: they don't grow great investigation habits. Most understudies do just what is important to accomplish their ideal imprints: they don't figure out how to stretch themselves as far as possible.

These types of learning would not do a musician much good. They would mean rehearsing just on appointed pieces, rehearsing just barely before a presentation, and not trying to handle the most testing pieces. The typical learning and study habits of most expressions understudies are not the reason for turning into a top entertainer. Procuring aptitudes in learning and continuous purposeful practice are, over the long haul, unmistakably more significant than learning content, composing papers or passing tests.

The equivalent applies to those of us required as educators and specialists. We invest undeniably more energy instructing and inquiring about as per habits we got years or decades back than we do refining or changing useless methods for working. This resembles a typist who perseveres in a since a long time ago settled yet wasteful two-fingered method as opposed to learning another one.

The high-yield composing system is worked around changing the normal habit for glut composing. This habit includes postponing composing until there is a major square of time or an approaching due date and after that spending long anguishing hours on an errand until it is finished. The thought is to supplant the gorging habit with a different one, brief every day composing. Research demonstrates that normal brief composition sessions are unmistakably progressively gainful - and that it tends to be amazingly difficult to change to the new habit.

Colleges as associations are based on examples of gathering behavior and formal methodology that can be analyzed as habits. It is conceivable to change hierarchical habits - however, this is a long way from simple. The potential prizes are colossal.

An aptitude that would be exceedingly significant to people and gatherings is having the option to analyze habits, choose attractive new ones, and continue to change to the new ones.

Authoritative Habits

In the wake of treating the habits of people, we go to associations. There is an intriguing record of how the chain store Target accumulates data about customers to envision what they are probably going to need to purchase, and afterward promote appropriately direct to every person. If their information anticipates that a client is anticipating her first youngster, Target can send promotions proper to each phase of the pregnancy. However, a few moms-to-be are insulted by an organization knowing clearly private realities about their lives, so Target keenly implants the individual significant advertisements among other apparently irregular ones, so the pitch is by all accounts individualized. However, every family unit on a road may get different promotions.

Strikingly, Target's top administration was unsettled about uncovering the organization's methods. This data is gotten from workers, and incorporates, in his notes, the organization's conventional reaction.

Regarding advertising, colleges are tenderfoots contrasted with Target and different organizations utilizing comparable strategies. Envision a college advancement conveyed through a few online lives that is inconspicuously custom fitted for every potential understudy's statistic attributes and individual conditions. That, to my brain, is certifiably not an attractive objective. More with regards to the conventional objectives of colleges would instruct, supervision and companion bolster versatile for individual understudies. Some dynamic US universities do this, with every understudy arranging a learning contract with a scholarly consultant. Australian colleges are dreadfully bureaucratized for anything like this to be practical.

Down to Earth Applications

Numerous readers will ask, "So how would I change my negative behavior patterns? How would I quit gorging and start working out? How would I quit tarrying and start dealing with my significant long haul extends?" The issue is, there is no enchantment arrangement. Obviously not – else we would all think about it as of now.

You have to do some handy examination to discover what the signs are for your habits and what activities you can use to supplant your standard behavior. Suppose you take a gander at your email before anything else, and check news stories around the globe, all of which winds up taking two or three hours and derailing from chipping away at your book. Indeed, you have delayed taking a shot at the book for as far back as year. You have to analysis to find the sign for your email habit, and trial with substitution exercises.

It is not as simple as it may appear. Changing habits should be possible, however, it is difficult, as health food nuts and smokers will let you know.

How Habits Work

Did you make another year's goals this year? Or then again more significantly, did you figure out how to stay with it? Possibly you chose to take up running or to eat all the more strongly. Some sort of moderately "minor" lifestyle change.

It may have appeared to be very direct on paper. Something that you thought was inside your compass. Also, it is useful for your wellbeing. Most likely that is sufficient inspiration?

Be that as it may, the issue is, it isn't just about inspiration. It is about habits. Furthermore, that is an entire other ball game. An entirely different neural hardware that you need to break into. Revamp.

Also, this neural habit hardware to you needs to modify-situated in a piece of your cerebrum called the basal ganglia – is hard-wired for automaticity. It is your programmed pilot circuit. The one that approaches its day by day business without you expecting to ponder it. Something that is extraordinarily helpful on one hand as it opens up your intuition time for other increasingly significant contemplations of the day. In any case, inconceivably disappointing then again on the grounds that it makes these habits extremely difficult to change.

How Do Habits Work?

Researchers have identified a "habit cycle" which clarifies how habits work. There are three components to the cycle – a sign, a daily practice, and a reward. Your mind sees a prompt, possibly something in your environment, and this sets off a specific daily practice. An activity or behavior that you do. Taking part in this normal gives you some sort of pleasurable experience. A reward for your cerebrum.

For instance, perhaps your morning course to work takes you past a specific bistro (the sign).

Each time you see the bistro, you go in a purchase an espresso and a (delightful however undesirable) biscuit (the daily schedule).

Yummy. (The Reward).

Rehash throughout the days, weeks ahead and hello presto you have a habit. A habit that is possibly difficult to break. A biscuit and espresso needing that starts the moment you foresee your voyage to work.

Also, it is your basal ganglia which are engaged with connecting your activities with these prizes after some time. It takes over from different pieces of your cerebrum which were associated with the underlying basic leadership procedure to proceed to purchase that first espresso and biscuit.

Also, when it is given over to the basal ganglia, that is the point at which it has quit turning into a "simply this once" sort of activity and rather is making a course for turning into a full-fledged habit. Programmed. Instilled into your neural wiring. Also, happening without appropriate conference with different areas of your cerebrum, for example, your prefrontal cortex, concerning whether this truly is the best strategy.

And this makes habits hard to break.

Upgrading Habits

In any case, one stunt with attempting to get out from under an unfortunate habit is in reality not to attempt to quit doing it. It is to update it.

If you simply stop it, at that point you are forestalling the mind getting the reward it needs. Also, that makes longings which are difficult to disregard. Making you backslide.

Upgrading the habit is an inconspicuous methodology. Less without any weaning period. More gradual steps.

Take the above case of snatching and espresso and (unfortunate) biscuit while in transit to work. You could overhaul the prompt by taking a different course to work. Overhaul the everyday practice by having some espresso before you get down to business, or when you get the chance to work so you don't lift one up (and the related biscuit) while in transit to work. Change the reward, so you incorporate something scrumptious (however more advantageous) for your work area breakfast to make up for the absence of early morning biscuit.

Your body and mind are as yet getting what they need, however in a way that is better for you. Fulfills that New Year's goals which is still pretty much sticking on. What's more, you didn't even truly need to quit any pretense of anything.

Obviously, a few habits are simpler to break than others. What's more, when they include physiological reactions which edge nearer to habit (liquor, nicotine, sugar, caffeine) you are probably going to be in for an extreme ride. Managing the related withdrawal side effects. Certainly not a change that can occur incidentally.

Also, there is no recipe for to what extent it takes individuals to change a habit. A few specialists state it takes 66 days to shape another habit. In any case, it is close to home. Furthermore, it relies upon the habit you are attempting to change. So take the time that you need.

In any case, that is sufficient about close to home habits. Shouldn't something be said about purchaser habits?

Useful for Business

All things considered, habits make shoppers unsurprising. They are amazing drivers of rehash behavior. Also, they happen throughout the day, consistently. Not exactly mind perusing. Be that as it may, the following best thing – behavior perusing.

Habits mean you can work out individuals' examples of behavior. Foresee how they will act later on. Furthermore, plan your items likewise.

Fitting them to the spot, the time and the mentality of the customer you are attempting to speak to. Expanding the probability that they will lock-in. Buy. Sign up.

Habit Disturbance

However, if you are needing to discharge another item into the market which may expect customers to change a habit, you likewise need to think cautiously.

Take the case of the ongoing presentation of in-shower lotions where you need to saturate in the shower, instead of after it. Truly, it is another item that requires a difference inhabit, however, it likewise fits in with a present habit (scrubbing down) so the prompt and the routine are as of now shaped. Furthermore, the reward is possibly more noteworthy by sparing your time and exertion.

Subsequently, it is a generally simple habit change to present. Problematic. Yet, not very problematic.

Yet, be careful. Regardless of whether you figure out how to get individuals to shape another habit you need to recall that the former one isn't eradicated. It is as yet sneaking there out of sight. Trusting that that snapshot of shortcoming will raise its revolting head.

Another item dispatch from a contender enticing your buyers back.

Or on the other hand, a scrumptious new biscuit flavor to attempt.

Identifying Your Good Habits

We, people, are animals of habit, along these lines growing great habits ought to be basic – right! All things considered, not generally. The issue is that we get truly happy with doing things a similar way every single day. We frequently absentmindedly adhere to a day by day schedule without thinking about the outcome or viability of it. Why change?

Tragically, not the majority of our habits are solid, or great. If we are in the habit of returning home after work every day and going after a mixed beverage to unwind as opposed to jumping on the treadmill to release pressure, it will antagonistically influence our wellbeing.

Or then again, if, while staring at the TV at night we will in general nibble on chips and drink soft drink as opposed to chomping on veggies and tasting on organic product juice, it will at last lead to the result of weakness.

If we are in the habit of smoking to assuage pressure/uneasiness, or over-eating, or taking our dissatisfactions out on others, we should perceive these as habits worth changing, or wiping out. So where do we start?

Basic Steps to Develop Good Habits

1. **Utilize Perception and Assertions.**

    Representation and insistences are incredible for coordinating the new habit into your daily practice. While representation is a ground-breaking inspirational instrument and energizer, certifications program the subliminal with the correct outlook for building up another habit. Together they enable you to feel and envision yourself completing the right behaviors making it simpler to receive the new habit. Unquestionably growing great habits is simpler when utilizing perception and confirmations.

2. **Settle on the Choice, and After That the Responsibility, to Change.**

    Obviously, this is more difficult than one might expect. How often have we said to ourselves, "Indeed, I should practice more and eat better. Not to stress, I'll get around to it at some point or another?"

    Lamentably, stalling just makes it harder to change a negative behavior pattern. The more you put off making a move, particularly where wellbeing is concerned, the unhealthier you, or the circumstance, will get. A cognizant responsibility is important in light of the fact that that is the stuff to get the wheels of movement in real life.

3. Enroll Support from Family and Companions.

Tell individuals what you are attempting to achieve. Along these lines, they will comprehend if you need to leave behind the desert or take a stroll as opposed to halting at the bar in transit home. At the point when your companions realize you are not kidding about changing an unfortunate habit into a decent one, not exclusively will they help you steer away from allurements, they will give a shout out to you and give you good help. We as a whole need support in accomplishing our objectives!

4. Identify the Habit.

As referenced, more often than not we are never again aware of our habits, positive or negative, so the main thing we need do is turned out to be mindful. If that hack has been deteriorating, or if we become winded in the wake of strolling up a couple of stairs, all things considered, a negative behavior pattern (smoking, stationary lifestyle), or an absence of a decent habit (work out) is at fault. Perhaps our funds are in disorder, which implies that we've been in the habit for spending more than we acquire, or not rehearsing the great habit of keeping up a financial limit and adhering to it. It is an ideal opportunity to look at our habits!

5. Find Solid Approaches to Remunerate Yourself.

One reason we create numerous negative behavior patterns, in any case, is on the grounds that they make us feel better, regardless of whether it is simply briefly. The experience of inclination great is intended to alleviate or assuage us when we're focused on, discouraged, or out and out unwell. For instance, you may over-eat and feel great while doing it, yet then you feel twice as awful subsequently. The equivalent goes for smoking or drinking excessively. While you are in the demonstration you feel loose and issue free, notwithstanding, thereafter you feel regret and promise to stop - soon.

6. Devise an Arrangement.

Benjamin Franklin had an incredible arrangement for defeating his negative behavior patterns and supplanting them with great ones. He built up a procedure whereby he recorded 13 ethics he felt were significant in his life and afterward continued to take a shot at them. He concentrated on one excellence for each week overlook great habits a multi-week time frame. Before every week's over he believed he had aced the negative behavior pattern so he continued to the following one the next week.

During this procedure, he kept a diary of his prosperity with ethics. Since a portion of the excellences encouraged the obtaining of others, he put them in a specific request starting with moderation since "it will, in general, acquire that coolness and clearness of head, which is so fundamental where steady watchfulness was to be kept up."

This will function admirably for any individual who is attempting to build up another great habit - carefulness is in reality expected to ensure you stay with it! After balance he took a shot at quiet since learning could be best acquired "by the utilization of the ears than of the tongue."

7. Find Your Triggers and Deterrents.

If you don't have the foggiest idea what your triggers are, or if you are not ready for the unavoidable impediments, you will set yourself up for disappointment. So as to grow great habits, we should know about what our habits are. We all, in snapshots of shortcoming and defenselessness, need support or a discharge for our disappointments. Going after liquor, drugs, over-eating, or over-curing isn't the appropriate response.

If an undesirable episode happens at work, or an untidy traffic squabble happens in transit home, you need to locate a sound option in contrast to your standard method for managing it. We as a whole have terrible days, however, we need not fall back on unfortunate habits to lighten the pressure. In like manner, we can't give fatigue, a chance to anger, or tension be triggers for unfortunate propensities either. Search for solid methods for managing triggers and snags.

Along these lines, so as to limit tumbling off the wagon and slipping once more into old, negative habits, compensate yourself when you have progressed admirably. Treat yourself to another book, a film, a show, or new practice hardware. If you are lacking in real money, visit a companion you haven't seen for some time, go to the midtown craftsmanship exhibition, or appreciate a thin latte.

The brilliant advantage of growing great habits is that in the wake of doing them over and again, they before long become programmed. Anything you accomplish for quite a while and reliably enough, in the end, turns into a habit, and once it does, you never again need to place much exertion into it. Such is the magnificence of growing great habits.

Identifying Your Bad Habits

It is anything but difficult to consider habits falling into highly contrasting classifications — practicing great, gnawing your nails awful. Be that as it may, habits additionally sit on a continuum in our capacity to exercise command over them: Some are mellow, such as removing your shoes and dumping them in the lounge each night; others are moderate, such as having supper before the TV, or drinking an excess of when you go to a gathering; and afterward those that are solid and addictive — like smoking.

Habits become hard to break since they are profoundly wired, by steady redundancy, into our minds. Also, when you add delight to them — like you have with medications or pornography, for instance — the joy focuses of the midbrain get started up too.

In any case, habits are additional examples of behavior and it is the breaking of examples that is simply the way to bringing an end to the habits. As a rule, there is a reasonable trigger to begin the example. Here and there the triggers are enthusiastic — the needing a beverage or cigarette or nail-gnawing driven by pressure. Different occasions the trigger is all the more basically situational and natural: You consider the To be and love seat when you hit the front entryway, and now your mind draws an obvious conclusion, and having supper before the TV on the lounge chair isn't a long ways behind. All the more frequently it is a blend of both — the blend of social tension and the gathering condition prompts your heavier drinking.

In any case, these examples are likewise normally enveloped by bigger ones: This is the place schedules come to run our lives. Here is the place, when you hit the front entryway after work, the dumping the shoes, the getting a lager, the sitting before the TV with supper stream together absent much idea, similarly as your morning work-break consequently prompts you and your companion, Kate, heading outside and visiting while you each have your early in the day cigarette.

By and large, these standard behaviors are developmental savvy and for all intents and purposes great. They shield us from reevaluating the wheel of our day by day lives by settling on an endless number of choices throughout the day, which thus gives us more mind space to consider different things. The drawback of these being routine examples comes when those examples land more in the terrible segment than the great one.

So if you have habits you need to break, here are a few stages to kick you off:

- Characterize the solid behavior you need to change or create

- Getting more exercise or treating your beau better may sound incredible yet they give you to get a handle on onto. You have to take action breaking process by intuition as far as specific, possible behaviors — like not dumping your shoes in the family room however placing them in your wardrobe; not eating before the TV set at the lounge area table; going for a half-hour run five days per week; sending your beau a complimentary book once every day, as opposed to sending him nothing or negative ones. Drill down on the solid.

Identify the Triggers

The icebox might be a sufficient trigger to have you go for the brew once you hit the entryway, similarly as observing the lousy nourishment on the counter will when you get exhausted. Or then again it might be that flash of social tension that wrenches up the drinking when you think about an up and coming occasion with multiple individuals. By identifying your triggers, you have a method for pushing back and not having that autopilot kick in.

In any case, a few people have a difficult time doing this. If this is valid for you, that you have a difficult time realizing what genuinely triggers you, you can work in reverse — see, for instance, when you are longing for a beverage or gnawing your nails, and delayed down and utilize your familiarity with these behaviors sign to ask yourself: What is going on inwardly?

Build up a Substitute Arrangement

Getting out from under habits isn't tied in with halting yet substituting. Here is the place you thought of an arrangement for dealing with the gathering without drinking — getting a mocktail and balancing near to your great companion, as opposed to snatching a beverage and being with stayed with a lot of outsiders.

Manage the Triggers

Since we're needing to break designs, you currently need to take care of the triggers themselves. Here you proactively get the lousy nourishment or brew out the house, or when you understand, while driving home, that you are focused, and you intentionally sit in the vehicle and tune in to music that you like while sitting in the garage, or do a couple of minutes of profound breathing to unwind, instead of consequently walking into the risk zone of the kitchen.

Or on the other hand, if you are worried about your gorging during the evening, plan to bring two treats up to your room at 11 o'clock and resolve not to return down the stairs for the remainder of the night to shield you from winding up meandering around the kitchen all night and veering towards the kitchen. Or on the other hand so as to evade the allurement of web pornography, plan to unplug your PC when you return home and avoid gadgets, and rather settle in with that new book you got for your birthday, or call your mother, all to abstain from falling into your set daily practice.

The key here is mapping this out before that triggers get an opportunity to kick in.

Change the Bigger Example

Here we are extending the setting that encompasses the habit-design. Here you go to the rec center during your mid-day break since you realize the following work is too hard when you are so worn out. Or on the other hand, you understand you don't sit at the lounge area table for supper since it is so stacked down with papers and such, thus you have to begin by both keeping the table clear and preparing the table for supper before you leave for work.

By taking a gander at and changing the bigger example you are really not just making it simpler to handle the center habit, yet are working on practicing your self-discipline on littler, simpler example breaking behaviors. This can add to your feeling of strengthening.

Get Underpins

Get a running mate, or a gathering amigo, or somebody you can call, or an online discussion you can take advantage of when you those desires begin to kick in and you are battling. Converse with your companion about going to get a snappy mug of espresso together as opposed to remaining outside with your cigarettes. Go to AA gatherings.

Backing and Reward Yourself

Sooner or later in your endeavors to bring an end to a habit, you arrive at a point where you go: Why am I trying to battle with this? You feel disheartened, you believe you are sincerely making your life apparently harder and that there is little result.

This is ordinary, the depressed spot simultaneously, and you have to keep your focus on the big picture. In any case, you additionally need to ensure you work in as a result. Here you intentionally pat yourself on the back for eating at the table as opposed to the love seat, despite the fact that you will not promptly feel much improved. You take the cash you would spend on liquor or medications or cigarettes and spare it up to purchase something different you have constantly needed—another outfit, a top of the line small scale get-away. Once more, you sink into having people around you to give a shout out to you and help you understand what you are gaining ground and are in the correct way.

Use prompts

These are suggestions to enable you to break the example by making positive triggers and alarms to keep you on track: Putting your running shoes along the edge of your bed so you see them before anything else, or putting a caution on your telephone to leave for the exercise center, or checking in with yourself and measuring your feeling of anxiety in transit home before it gets excessively high and out of your control.

Be tenacious and tolerant

That is the name of the game, obviously: understanding that it will require some investment for the new cerebrum associations with kick in, for the old mind firings to quiet down, for new examples to supplant the old. Try not to thump yourself for slip-ups or use them as reasons for stopping. Take it one day at the time.

Consider getting proficient assistance

If you have done as well as can be expected and you are as yet battling, think about looking for expert help. This might be a specialist who can recommend prescriptions for the fundamental tension and wretchedness, an advisor who can't just enable you to unwind the sources and drivers of your habits, yet additionally give some relentless help and responsibility.

While all habits are not made similarly, the all-encompassing objective is the equivalent, to be specific you take in charge of your life and being proactive instead of responsive, intentional as opposed to being routine.

Chapter 2 – Habits of Highly Effective People

Empowering People

We live in a culture that is shifting continuously. The sort of pioneer children of post-war America tried to be is different from the sort of pioneer Millennials and Generation X put their focus on.

The shift in authority style has to a great extent been a consequence of the shifting commercial center and what is expected of organizations to be aggressive. Twenty years back, it was about order and control-being unequivocal and definitive. The pioneer of the past was relied upon to have every one of the appropriate responses and guide their workers. Representatives must keep the guidelines, do what they were told, and pay their levy until they were elevated to a place of power.

At this time, satisfaction at work was a pipe dream. You were informed that if you keep your focus on the big picture - power and authority- - at that point, you would be "effective." But I'm not catching that's meaning? In this model, nobody is glad and flourishing. Direction and control make a situation where representatives are famished of self-governance and after that getting alcoholic on power once they get to the highest point of the stepping stool. Everything is out of equalization, and the organization endures.

Be that as it may, presently directing and controlling is clearing a path for an increasingly community-oriented method for driving. The market is requesting advancement at such a quick rate, that unlimited thoughts are required so as to contend. These unlimited thoughts can't just originate from a pioneer; however, they should originate from every other person included.

In this manner, the pith of administration is shifting from instructing everybody, to enabling others to think of the best and most brilliant thoughts that have never been idea of. How at that point do you enable individuals to be their best?

Here are six incredible ways you can start to have business accomplishment by helping your group be their best:

Live the behaviors that you need them to grasp.

Guiding different grown-ups isn't a successful inspiration system. When was the last time being determined what to do made you feel motivated and prepared to roll out genuine improvement? Likely never, in light of the fact that this is the most exceedingly terrible approach to get people to change. You realize what is profoundly viable? Exhibiting the behaviors, activities, and qualities you want to find in others. Nonetheless, this requires duty and order from you, the pioneer. You must be the individual you need your group to be.

Help Them Reveal Their Zone of Genius.

Your Zone of Genius is the crossing point of your inborn intellectual competence and your motivation. Your mental attitude is the manner by which your cerebrum naturally prefers to issue comprehend and process data. Your motivation is connected to what makes satisfaction for you and is associated with your brain research. Make sense of your most noteworthy life challenge- - the one thing that you generally adapt to the situation to help other people with. That is your Zone of Genius. At that point, you have the formula for interminable inspiration when you need it.

Give Your Group the Self-Governance to Do It All Alone.

Don't micromanage- - another inspiration executioner. Give individuals space. I have met endless CEOs that have moved to a Results-Only Work Environment. All CEOs detailed expanded inspiration and dedication. Give your kin more opportunity than you feel good with- - what appears the scariest activity some of the time is the most dominant. Your group will come back with results you can't envision.

Be a Supplier.

In his book Give and Take, Adam Grant takes note of that best individuals provide for others without contemplating receiving anything consequently. When you need to engage others, provide for them. Be liberal, and they will feel associated with you, increased in value by you, and motivated to do likewise.

Approach Them What Their Vision Is for Their Vocation or Employment.

A great many people don't have the foggiest idea of what their vision is for their profession or occupation. The significance of a dream is that it can manage you in snapshots of progress or in venture prioritization. Having your kin know the bearing they need to control themselves improves effectiveness as well as a simple method to guarantee they are figuring out how to inspire themselves.

Keep away from offering your group the responses. Or maybe, express the issue and let them think of the arrangement.

This is tied in with overseeing yourself. We frequently do things unwittingly and after that question why we are not getting the outcomes we need. Watch yourself all the more intently with regard to what you state to your group or others. It is safe to say that you are keeping away from instructing them? You should, yet this isn't simple. We live in a power-hungry society and it is simpler to utilize our capacity muscle, instruct others and use it as a chance to stroke our own personalities. This doesn't, notwithstanding, engage others to be their best.

At the point when individuals feel enabled, they put stock in themselves and their capacity to control their own and expert lives. Engaging others advances positive thinking and a "can-do" soul that completes things—quicker and better. Here are 10 hints for helping other people become all they are fit for being.

Try not to strive to be the focal point of consideration; share the spotlight and gathering achievement. Hoarding the spotlight generally creates disdain, while sharing makes certain to bring gratefulness and appreciation.

Give wholeheartedly of your time and consideration, without anticipating anything consequently. Companions and associates will, thus, feel acknowledged and return your liberality in kind.

Make a special effort to interface with new partners. Visit with them, welcome them out for an espresso; make them feel that they are a welcome, esteemed piece of the group.

Model positive character characteristics you have faith in. Others will pay heed and copy your words and activities.

If you are responsible for a gathering, let everybody know your worth their assessment. Energize the individuals who might be modest to shout out. Try not to put down anybody's commitments, regardless of whether you can't help contradicting those specific ideas.

Listen eagerly. Try not to lose the center when somebody addresses you. Take a gander at them and gesture to show you are following the discussion. This will urge the other individual to keep on sharing their thoughts.

Offer individuals the two most underestimated words in the English language: "much obliged." They show others that you saw their assistance or potentially capacities and are thankful.

Give direct reports of self-governance. Give them a chance to come up with their very own thoughts and answers. Individuals who feel responsible for their decisions more joyful, progressively satisfied—and increasingly beneficial. Act toward others as you would have others act toward you—with benevolence, thought and regard.

Give genuine compliments, regardless of whether you are applauding the nature of somebody's work, their assistance with a task, or another outfit.

Foresight and Focus

What's to come is too imperative to possibly be left to risk. Previously, organizations outlasted individuals. Presently, it is regularly a different way.

Mohist rhetoric can be used to counter the spread of misinformation by government agencies because it offers a basis for 'universal love' and submission to the 'will of Heaven.' Mohist rhetoric is a Chinese philosophy that emphasizes the importance of God (the Lord on High) and universal love is radically changing behavior in society. This philosophy was conceived by Mozi through his teachings, and it emphasizes practicality and equality in society. One of the fundamental aspects of the philosophy is that it emphasizes a meritocratic society that is led by a virtuous monarch and officials who have been appointed on the basis of their abilities to handle the responsibilities rather than social status. The philosophy is particularly critical of the excesses of society, such as the Confucian funeral rites that used a significant amount of funds that would be better spent in society.

This rhetoric can be used to counter the spread of misinformation by government agencies by utilizing the Mohist advice in the selection of appropriate leaders. Mohist rhetoric emphasizes selecting leaders based on their skills and capabilities rather than their background, and this will go a long way in ensuring those in charge of information do not spread misinformation. Similarly, Mohist rhetoric points to the importance of a superior being in society, God; thus, all actions undertaken by a government agency should incorporate the teachings and instructions of God when dispatching information. Thus, all action taken by the government should take into consideration 'the will of Heaven' and ensure that all activities undertaken is per God's laws. Therefore, this paper will provide information on the specific ways that the Mohist rhetoric can be used to counter the spread of misinformation by government agencies.

Mohist reasoning was characterized by specific principles that provided its followers with a basic understanding of how to conduct themselves in society. One of the critical characteristics of Mohist reasoning was that there should be an emphasis on frugality and utility among the population. This means that all the resources in society should be coordinated and used towards advancing the progress of the community and enhancing the welfare of each individual. Therefore, all activities taking place in society should take into consideration the general progress expected for the community without bias.

The condemnation of luxury and waste in society is also another critical characteristic of Mohist reasoning. The principles of this ideology are that luxury in society should not be tolerated, particularly at the expense of the general activities that will promote progress in the community. Individuals in positions of authority should not live their lives in luxury while the rest of the population mires in poverty. In the same light, waste should also not be tolerated because it is necessary to bring together all the resources of the community towards bettering the welfare of each individual. Therefore, luxury and waste are fundamental aspects of the community that must be avoided for the sake of a better tomorrow.

Another important characteristic of Mohist reasoning is a utilitarian approach in the management of the affairs of the community. 'Concerned with the common people, they propelled a utilitarian political-social philosophy, directed towards the material well-being of all. All actions taken in society by figures of authority must recognize the benefits of every member in the community as opposed to single groups of individuals. This means that in a Mohist society, good morals encompass those actions that will be favorable to the majority of people. Therefore, this crucial characteristic of Mohist reasoning provides an emphasis on impartial care for each member of the community regardless of their social status.

Reverence for God (the Lord on High) as another important characteristic of Mohist reasoning that guided the decisions and actions taken by Mohists at the time. The Mohists believed that all life originated from God, and that having reverence and respect for him was the only way society could progress. The Mohists also emphasized worshipping traditional deities and maintaining the importance of a supreme being as being an important aspect of Chinese culture. Therefore, this characteristic enabled each individual to respect each individual on the basis of the same love that God has for everybody.

Mohist reasoning can be used as a tool of argumentation to counter common misinformation tactics found today. First, Mohist reasoning involves the belief that figures of authority in society should be appointed to such posts based on their abilities to get the job done rather than social status. This means that the leaders in society will have gone through extensive screening processes to ensure that they are morally upright individuals trusted by a majority of the public. Therefore, this approach can be used to counter the spread of misinformation by ensuring that there are credible leaders selected by the majority to ensure actions taken by the government work in the best interest of the public.

Similarly, Mohist reasoning can be used to tackle the challenge of misinformation in the present-day world by condemning the luxuries and wastes of society. A luxurious society will be indifferent to the information they receive as long as it does not affect the luxury, and this promotes the spread of misinformation. Also, a wasteful society will be comprised of misinformation because most people will be convinced not to think about the waste that is actually being generated around them. As Chris Fraser has pointed out, drawing distinctions in this way is the functional equivalent, in Mohist thought, of making a judgment or forming a belief. The ability to draw the distinctions correctly is knowledge. Therefore, employing Mohist reasoning to the conduct of life and society to manage luxury and waste in a systematic way will help counter the spread of misinformation associated with these ills of society.

The utilitarian approach of Mohist reasoning can also be used to counter the spread of misinformation by highlighting the fact that all information should benefit every individual. An important characteristic of misinformation is that the action is perpetuated for the benefit of only a few while the majority have to live with a lie. Therefore, a utilitarian approach emphasizes sharing true information with as many people in society as possible with the desired impact being favorable to the members of the community.

Building Strong Relationships

The most significant single fixing in the equation of achievement is realizing how to coexist with individuals. — Theodore Roosevelt

One of the most significant encounters we can have in our lives is the association we have with other individuals. Positive and strong connections will assist us with feeling more advantageous, more joyful, and increasingly happy with our lives. So here are a couple of tips to assist you with developing progressively positive and solid connections in all parts of your life:

Ethics and morals describe the proper ways of governing human behavior that guarantee everybody lives in peace and harmony. Observing the codes of ethics is an integral part of society today because it ensures that there is equity as well as justice. These rules specify the manner in which people should live and interact with one another without any discrimination or favor against other individuals. There are various scopes of ethics and morals that govern how people live with each other and manage the resources around them. The concept of ethics can apply to a different set of individuals in society and the surrounding environment.

Ethically, people should live with respect and jovial regard for one another to ensure that there is no bias. Each person on earth is equal and has the right to share the freedoms of everybody else. This means that behaving in a moral manner does not anger or limit the opportunities of another person in a purposeful way. Instead, there is careful regard for the interests of other individuals as well as the welfare of the entire community. This careful approach towards minding the wellbeing of the surrounding people constitutes ethical behavior.

The laws that govern countries and nations on earth also have a significant influence in shaping the views on ethics and morals. The laws provide definite rules and regulations that determine the manner in which people will interact with one another. The laws are very clear on the activities that have the consideration of being legal or not. Therefore, those individuals who act outside the bounds of the law are liable for punishment because their actions were not ethical. Remaining within the boundaries of the law is essential in ensuring there is a high level of accountability among everybody. This reduces the chances of disharmony and quarrels because everybody has the perception of being on a level field with other people in the community.

Religions that exist in the world are also very influential in shaping the views on morals and ethics. This is because religious teachings provide a basis for the best human behavior and positive activities that assure the best out of everybody. Religion is very strict in providing details about how people should live with one another because it distinguishes good behavior from the bad. Thus, acceptable behavior according to religion is ethical and moral because it does not negatively influence the surrounding society.

The manner in which people interact with the environment is also a significant influence on the views of morals and ethics. It is vital that human beings mind the surrounding environment and ensure its existence for years to come because it is the most ethical action to perform. Preserving the environment is a vital concept because human life firmly depends on the wellbeing of the natural ecosystems. Thus, it is ethical behavior to conserve and manage the environment to ensure its virility in supporting life and being available for future generations, as well.

In line with the subject matter of Prey, there are a number of contrasts as well as comparisons with today's technology. The book by Michael Crichton, Prey, talks about the technological advancements that might shape the earth one day. The plot of the story takes shape through a woman who is working in the nanotechnology department section of her company. She quickly rises to prominence mainly because her husband loses his job and becomes a sit-in partner. Thus, the wife has to focus all her energy on her career in order to support her family and achieve her interests, as well.

Thus, one of the main contrasts of the subject matter of Prey with today's technology is the existence of robots. The storyline talks about the protagonist looking for an appropriate technological strategy to develop the latest machine. Her work is top secret and even her husband has no idea what she is working on. Her isolation in developing this technology causes her husband to believe that she is having an extramarital affair when she is away. But the reality is that the development of this technology does not compare with anything present in today's society, meaning that she needs a lot of time out to develop it.

The development of robots is a dominant feature of the work by Michael Crichton. The story is very futuristic as it provides details of the manufacture and development of these machines and incorporating them in society. This technology currently does not exist in today's world mainly because it is still in its initial stages of development. Thus, this disambiguation provides an insight into the possible future of the world with the incorporation of robots into various operations. This technology has significant advancements that highlight the main differences with today's technology.

In addition to the differences in the level of technology in Crichton's book and today's world, there is a lot of information about genetic engineering. Relatively new to the world of technology, genetic engineering involves altering the genes within different species of animals and human beings to achieve biological balances. Genetic engineering is a sensitive topic because it goes against the norms of society, especially religious opinion. This is because the purposes and processes of genetic engineering have close links to the creation of beings, a concept that only has an association with God and other superior beings.

Thus, the comprehensive explanations about genetic engineering serve to open up a future world where anything might be possible. This obvious difference in the capabilities of human beings in the future highlights the major contrast of Crichton's book with the current technology. The ability to develop and alter genetic material in order to create other beings is a concept that scientists can only dream about in today's world. However, there are moderate introductions of genetic engineering in today's technology, but the levels that Crichton talks about in his novel are far ahead of today's time. This is one of the contrasting issues in Crichton's novel of today's technology and that of the future.

Another essential issue in discussion in the novel is the issues surrounding artificial intelligence. There is a lot of similarity of this technology with the current achievements in today's world. This is because several scientists around the world are already practicing artificial intelligence to induce life and ensure appropriate biological balances. Thus, artificial intelligence usually involves the manual combination of genetic factors in both animals and human beings that leads to life. This technology offers a suitable method of controlling populations within a given region because it offers the ability to add life to the planet.

The book by Michael Crichton offers some similarities as well as differences in the development and application of artificial intelligence. In today's technology, using artificial intelligence for biological factors has a number of disadvantages as well as advantages. There is a lot of room for error because the development of the technology is still ongoing. This means that there is still a lot of room for error as there is the possibility that it will not work. This means that there is still room for improving the current levels of technology surrounding artificial intelligence.

However, according to the descriptions of Michael Crichton in his novel, Prey, the future will hold some of the most significant changes to artificial intelligence. Among the major details in the novel include the accuracy and appropriateness of artificial intelligence in regulating life on earth. As a result of this technology, it is possible for scientists to schedule the creation of human life through appropriate scientific techniques. This futuristic technology is responsible for increasing life manually both in animals and human beings, leaving very little room for error. In addition to the knowledge from genetic engineering and nanotechnology, it is possible for scientists to rapidly create new life in shocking precision.

Therefore, the technological advancements of the future are very different from the current technology in today's world. But according to Crichton's novel, human beings will eventually reach the stage where they played almost the same role as God. His frightening ability to determine the creation of life and the control of several biological factors brings up the issues of ethics and morality. This is because, according to the present world, it is ethical to fully obey God, avoid blasphemy and take up some of his roles, like the creation of life.

Here are also other similarities and differences in the technology within Crichton's novel and today's world. In respect to the additional knowledge human being possess in the creation of life, artificial life soon becomes an issue as there are several beings on Earthborn this way. Artificial life is a controversial issue because lifeforms represent the work of human beings rather than a superior being. Even scientists acknowledge that the origin of life must have been from an external force with superior powers than the ordinary person. Thus, the ability to create life raises a lot of questions and questions the ethical and moral fiber of artificial life.

In addition to the biological focus of enhancing technology, there are significant developments in the field of scientific computing. In the future, computers become more complex and technical to use as they acquire attributes that are closer to the human brain. The power and complexity of these computers allow for their durability because they use alternative energy sources. This means that they offer a larger and better life span than today's technology where only a few computers have the power to match.

One of the significant additions to the technology surrounding computers is a battery with the capability to survive for a very long time. This allows the computer to perform complex operations that bear similarity to the operations of the brain. This raises ethical as well as moral questions in today's world because only God can biologically create a complex organ capable of complex operations.

This perception seems to be at the back foot of Crichton's novel as he goes on to explain the complexity of the evolution of computers. The result of this evolution is a very technical machine that does not correspond to the modern technology in today's world.

The purchasing world and scientific advances in computers is the right approach when seeking to know more about Crichton's technology descriptions. It is appropriate for the individual to do some research into the market as well as the available products. It is one thing knowing the type of watch to buy; it is another thing getting an appropriate dealer to help. Thus, doing early research on the internet about the technology will enable the individual to open up their options. This way, it will be possible to find the right professionals who will sell the right product at a good price.

Some of the main features include the option to come in a digital or the traditional model. This is essential because the market consists of customers with different tastes and preferences, thus drawing relevance on stocking up with several options. The watches have waterproof installations in addition to high power batteries that guarantee the watch remains active for a long period of time. Additionally, another interesting feature of the watch is a classic, leather strap option that allows the user to get the best possible product. These features enhance the watch and enable it to compete strongly within the market.

One of the main advantages of purchasing this watch is its long-lasting battery that enables the watch to remain durable for years. A steady battery ensures that the watch does not stop functioning within a short time. Another advantage of this watch is that it is practical as it can be used by anybody. Its waterproof abilities enable it to be practical for use both in the office as well as manual labor activities. Lastly, purchasing this watch will allow the user to access a one year guarantee that allows them to get their money back if they are not satisfied with the product.

One of the disadvantages of this watch is its relative pricing within the market. In comparison to most other watches within this class, it is pricey and is likely only to attract a few interested customers. In addition to this, its main features and appearance bear resemblance to other products within the market. This means that the consumer has a wide variety of options to select from and can easily look over the novel, Prey. Lastly, the leather option is an additional extra that the customer will have to pay for, meaning that they will spend more money to get the best watch.

Despite the disadvantages, the watch is modern and appealing for the current generation, incorporating the latest changes. In the dark, the watch-hands as well as the figures of the digital watch are luminous and allow it to be used in the darkest scenario. The styling and craft behind the final product makes it beautiful to wear and appealing to onlookers. Therefore, it is a pleasing product to have and likely to improve in value in the future due to its aesthetic appeal. Thus, customers should look no further if they want to fully benefit from the futuristic technological advancements.

Thus, the major ethical discussions and debates surrounding the technological descriptions in Crichton's novel mainly revolve around religious factors. Religion offers a significant basis for developing ethical and moral opinions in today's world, thus offering an excellent description of some of the dilemmas in the book. Religion is very clear and categorical on the origins of human beings and all other life on earth. It specifically states that human beings are the product of the work of God and only He can regulate, end and create new life.

Thus, Crichton's descriptions of artificial life and the complex advancements in the scientific world create ethical dilemmas because most people believe that life comes from a superior being. Therefore, the main ethical issues in discussion, in this case, are the capabilities and expertise of the human being in relation to God. The reader of this novel will find it difficult to believe that human beings will advance to a level where they can regulate life on Earth. This creates a lot of controversy because today's technology s nowhere near achieving these scientific fetes.

The description of the issues surrounding ethics in today's world is that man has a limit towards achieving the success of God. Thus, the constant reference to modern technology that rivals the power of God is the most significant ethical issue in discussion. There is a lot of association of a lack of ethics in the future of the world as a result of the rapid advancements in technology. Therefore, the novel, Prey, offers an insight into the role of technology in determining the fate of human beings in the future world.

Faith and Commitment

Would you be able to recognize a decent relationship? Obviously, no one realizes what truly goes on between any couple, yet many years of scientific examination into adoration, sex and connections have instructed us that various behaviors can foresee when a couple is on strong ground or set out toward harried waters. Great connections don't occur without any forethought. They take responsibility, bargain, pardoning and a large portion of all — exertion. Continue perusing for the most recent in relationship science, fun tests and accommodating tips to enable you to manufacture a more grounded bond with your accomplice.

Love and Romance

Beginning to look all starry eyed at is the simple part. The test for couples is the manner by which to revive the flames of sentiment every now and then and develop the develop, confiding in adoration that is the sign of an enduring relationship.

- What's Your Love Style?

- When you state "I adore you," I'm not catching your meaning?

- Sentimental: Based on energy and sexual fascination

- Closest Friends: Fondness and profound love

- Consistent: Practical sentiments dependent on shared qualities, monetary objectives, religion and so forth.

- Energetic: Feelings evoked by tease or feeling tested

- Possessive: Jealousy and fixation

- Unselfish: Nurturing, consideration, and sacrifice

Specialists have discovered that the adoration we feel in our most dedicated connections is ordinarily a mix of a few different types of affection. In any case, frequently, two individuals in a similar relationship can have altogether different adaptations of how they characterize love. Scientists give the case of a man and lady eating. The server plays with the lady; however, the spouse doesn't appear to notice, and discussions about replacing the oil in her vehicle. The wife is vexed her better half isn't envious. The spouse feels his additional work isn't valued.

What does this have to do with affection? The man and lady each characterize love differently. For him, love is functional and is best appeared by steady motions like vehicle upkeep. For her, affection is possessive, and a desirous reaction by her significant other makes her vibe esteemed.

Understanding what makes your accomplice feel adored can enable you to explore struggle and set sentiment back into your relationship. You and your accomplice can take the Love Style test from Dr. Hatkoff and discover how every one of you characterizes love. If you become familiar with your accomplice inclines toward envy, ensure you see when somebody is playing with that person. If your accomplice is handy in affection, see the numerous little ways the person in question shows love by dealing with regular needs.

Sentimental love has been known as a "characteristic compulsion" since it initiates the mind's reward focus - strikingly the dopamine pathways related to illicit drug use, liquor, and betting. Be that as it may, those equivalent pathways are likewise connected with oddity, vitality, center, learning, inspiration, delight and desiring. No big surprise we feel so empowered and roused when we begin to look all starry eyed at!

Yet, we as a whole realize that sentimental, energetic love blurs somewhat after some time, and (we trust) develops into an increasingly mollified type of submitted love. All things being equal, numerous couples long to revive the flashes of early romance. Be that as it may, is it conceivable?

Explore new territory and different – and ensure you do it together. New encounters enact the cerebrum's reward framework, flooding it with dopamine and norepinephrine. These are similar mind circuits that are lighted in early sentimental love. Regardless of whether you take a ceramics class or go on a wilderness boating trip, initiating your dopamine frameworks while you are as one can help bring back the fervor you felt on your first date. In investigations of couples, Dr. Aron has discovered that accomplices who normally share new encounters report more prominent lifts in conjugal satisfaction than the individuals who just share charming however natural encounters.

Analyze Your Passion Level

The brain research educator Elaine Hatfield has recommended that the adoration we feel right off the bat in a relationship is different than what we feel later. Right off the bat, love is "enthusiastic," which means we have sentiments of exceptional yearning for our mate. Longer-term connections create "companionate love," which can be depicted as a profound friendship, and solid sentiments of duty and closeness.

Where does your relationship arrive on the range of affection? The Passionate Love Scale, created by Dr. Hatfield, of the University of Hawaii, and Susan Sprecher, a brain science and humanism educator at Illinois State University, can enable you to measure the energy level of your relationship. When you see where you stand, you can begin taking a shot at infusing more energy into your association. Note that while the scale is broadly utilized by relationship analysts who study love, the test is in no way, shape or form the last word on the strength of your relationship. Take it for entertainment only and let the inquiries rouse you to converse with your accomplice about enthusiasm. All things considered, no one can really tell where the discussion may lead.

Sex

For most couples, the more sex they have, the more joyful the relationship.

The Amount Sex Are You Having?

How about we start with the uplifting news. Submitted couples truly have more sex than every other person. Try not to trust it? While the facts demonstrate that solitary individuals can amuse you with accounts of insane sexual scenes, recall that solitary individuals additionally experience long droughts. A report in 2017 found that 15 percent of men and 27 percent of ladies revealed they hadn't engaged in sexual relations in the previous year. What's more, 9 percent of men and 18 percent of ladies state they haven't had intercourse in five years. The primary components related to a sexless life are more seasoned age and not being hitched. So whether you are having dedicated or hitched sex once every week, when a month or only six times each year, the truth of the matter is that there is still somebody who might be listening having less sex than you. What's more, if you are one of those individuals NOT having intercourse, this will brighten you up: Americans who are not having intercourse are similarly as glad as their explicitly dynamic partners.

The No-Sex Marriage

For what reason do a few couples sizzle while others fail? Social researchers are reading no-sex relationships for intimations about what can turn out badly seeing someone.

It is evaluated that 15 percent of wedded couples have not had intercourse with their life partner over the most recent a half year to one year. Some sexless relationships began with next to no sex. Others in sexless relationships state labor or an undertaking prompted an easing back and in the end halting of sex. Individuals in sexless relationships are commonly not so much glad but rather more prone to have considered separation than the individuals who have ordinary sex with their mate or submitted accomplice.

If you have a low-sex or no-sex marriage, the most significant advance is to see a specialist. A low sex drive can be the aftereffect of a therapeutic issue (low testosterone, erectile brokenness, menopause, or misery) or it very well may be a reaction of a prescription or treatment. A few researchers estimate that developing the utilization of antidepressants like Prozac and Paxil, which can discourage the sex drive, might contribute an expansion in sexless relationships.

While a few couples in sexless relationships are cheerful, actually the more sex several has, the more joyful they are as one. It is difficult to revive a marriage that has abandoned sex for quite a long time, however, it very well may be finished. If you can't live in a sexless marriage however you need to remain wedded, see a specialist, see an advisor and start conversing with your accomplice.

Here is a portion of the means specialists prescribe to recover a sexless marriage in the room:

- Converse with one another about your wants.
- Have a ton of fun together and share new encounters to remind yourself how you began to look all starry eyed at.
- Clasp hands. Contact. Embrace.

Engage in sexual relations regardless of whether you would prefer not to. Numerous couples find that if they constrain themselves to engage in sexual relations, soon it doesn't move toward becoming work and they recollect that they like sex. The body reacts with a surge of cerebrum synthetics and different changes that can help.

Keep in mind that there is no set point for the perfect measure of sex in a marriage. The appropriate measure of sex is the sum that satisfies the two accomplices.

A Prescription for a Better Sex Life

If your sexual coexistence has disappeared, it can require some investment and exertion to get it in the groove again. The best arrangement is moderately basic, however very difficult for some, couples: Start discussing sex.

Take care of business: Have sex, regardless of whether you are not in the state of mind. Sex triggers hormonal and substance reactions in the body, and regardless of whether you are not in the disposition, odds are you will arrive rapidly once you start.

Set aside a few minutes for sex: Busy accomplices regularly state they are unreasonably occupied for sex, yet strikingly, truly bustling individuals appear to discover time to have illicit relationships. The truth of the matter is, sex is useful for your relationship. Make it a need.

Talk: Ask your accomplice what the person needs. Shockingly, this is by all accounts the greatest test couples face with regards to rebooting their sexual experiences.

The initial two proposals are plain as day, however how about we set aside some effort to investigate the third step: conversing with your accomplice about sex. Dr. Hatfield of the University of Hawaii is one of the pioneers of relationship science. She built up the Passionate Love scale we investigated before in this guide. Whenever Dr. Hatfield directed a progression of meetings with people about their sexual wants, she found that people share considerably more practically speaking than they understand, they simply tend not to discuss sex with one another. Here's a straightforward exercise dependent on Dr. Hatfield's examination that could hugely affect your sexual coexistence:

Discover Two Bits of Paper and Two Pens.

Presently, plunk down with your accomplice so every one of you can record five things you need a greater amount of during sex with your accomplice. The appropriate responses shouldn't be nitty-gritty sex acts (in spite of the fact that that is fine if it is critical to you). In a perfect world, your answers should concentrate on behaviors you want - being garrulous, sentimental, delicate, trial or courageous.

If you resemble the couples in Dr. Hatfield's examination, you may find that you share undeniably more for all intents and purpose as far as sexual wants than you understand. Here are the appropriate responses Dr. Hatfield's couples gave.

How about we see what couples shared for all intents and purposes. The two accomplices needed enchantment, guidelines, and experimentation.

The fundamental difference for people is the place sexual want starts. Men needed their spouses to start sex all the more frequently and be less restrained in the room. Yet, for ladies, behavior outside the room additionally made a difference. They needed their accomplice to be hotter, useful in their lives, and they needed love and compliments both all through the room.

Remaining Faithful

People can prepare themselves to ensure their connections and raise their sentiments of responsibility.

Would you be able to Predict Infidelity?

At whatever year around 10 percent of wedded individuals — 12 percent of men and 7 percent of ladies — state they have engaged in sexual relations outside their marriage. The moderately low paces of yearly duping cover the far higher pace of lifetime conning. Among individuals, more than 60, around one out of four men and one of every seven ladies concede they have ever conned.

Various investigations in the two creatures and people recommend that there might be a hereditary part to disloyalty. While science presents a convincing defense that there is some hereditary part to tricking, we likewise realize that hereditary qualities are not fate. What's more, until there is a quick quality test to decide the betrayal danger of your accomplice, the discussion about the hereditary qualities of disloyalty isn't especially helpful to anybody.

There are some character attributes known to be related to bamboozling. A report in The Archives of Sexual Behavior found that two attributes anticipated hazard for unfaithfulness in men. Men who are effectively stimulated (called "affinity for sexual excitation") and men who are excessively worried about sexual execution disappointment are bound to swindle. The discovering originates from an investigation of almost 1,000 people. In the example, 23 percent of men and 19 percent of ladies announced consistently undermining an accomplice.

For ladies, the primary indicators of unfaithfulness were relationship bliss (ladies who are upset in their association are twice as prone to cheat) and being explicitly out-of-synchronize with their accomplice (a circumstance that makes ladies multiple times as liable to cheat as ladies who feel explicitly perfect with their accomplices).

Ensure Your Relationship

1. Plan Ahead for Temptation. People can create adapting procedures to remain devoted to an accomplice.

    A progression of unordinary studies driven by John Lydon, an analyst at McGill University in Montreal, saw how individuals in a submitted relationship respond even with allurement. In one investigation, profoundly dedicated wedded people were solicited to rate the engaging quality from individuals of the contrary sex in a progression of photographs. As anyone might expect, they gave the most noteworthy appraisals to individuals who might commonly be seen as alluring.

Afterward, they were demonstrated comparable pictures and told that the individual was keen on gathering them. In that circumstance, members reliably gave those photos lower scores than they had the first run through around.

When they were pulled in to somebody who may undermine the relationship, they appeared to intuitively let themselves know, "He's not all that good." "The more dedicated you are," Dr. Lydon stated, "the less alluring you discover other individuals who undermine your relationship."

Other McGill concentrates affirmed differences in how people respond to such dangers. In one, alluring entertainers or on-screen characters were acquired to play with study members in a lounge area. Afterward, the members were posed inquiries about their connections, especially how they would react to an accomplice's awful behavior, such as being late and neglecting to call.

Men who had quite recently been being a tease were less lenient of the theoretical terrible behavior, recommending that the alluring entertainer had immediately worn down their responsibility. In any case, ladies who had been being a tease were bound to pardon and to rationalize the man, recommending that their prior being a tease had set off a defensive reaction when examining their relationship.

"We figure the men in these examinations may have had responsibility, however, the ladies had the emergency course of action — the appealing elective sets off the alert," Dr. Lydon said. "Ladies certainly code that as a danger. Men don't."

The investigation likewise took a gander at whether an individual can be prepared to oppose enticement. The group provoked male understudies who were in dedicated dating connections to envision running into an alluring lady on an end of the week when their sweethearts were away. A portion of the men were then approached to build up an alternate course of action by filling in the sentence "When she approaches me, I will _____ to secure my relationship."

Since the specialists morally couldn't acquire a genuine lady to go about as an enticement, they made a computer-generated simulation game in which two out of four rooms included subliminal pictures of an alluring lady. A large portion of the men who had worked on opposing enticement avoided the rooms with alluring ladies; however, among men who had not polished obstruction, two out of three inclined toward the allurement room.

Obviously, it is a lab study and doesn't generally disclose to us what may occur in reality with a genuine lady or man enticing you to stray from your relationship. Be that as it may, if you stress you may be defenseless against allurement on an excursion for work, practice obstruction by reminding yourself the means you will take to keep away from enticement and ensure your relationship.

2. Keep Your Relationship Interesting. Researchers hypothesize that your degree of duty may rely upon how much an accomplice improves your life and expands your

perspectives — an idea that Dr. Aron, the Stony Brook brain science educator, calls "self-extension."

To quantify this quality, couples are posed a progression of inquiries: How much does your accomplice give a wellspring of energizing encounters? What amount has realizing your accomplice made you a superior individual? What amount do you consider your to be as an approach to grow your very own abilities?

The Stony Brook specialists directed tests utilizing exercises that animated self-development. A few couples were given ordinary errands, while others participated in a senseless exercise where they were integrated and requested to creep on mats, driving forth chamber with their heads. The investigation was fixed so the couples bombed as far as possible on the initial two attempts, yet scarcely made it on the third, bringing about much festival.

Couples were given relationship tests when the trial. The individuals who had partaken in the difficult action posted more noteworthy increments in adoration and relationship fulfillment than the individuals who had not experienced triumph together. The scientists estimate that couples who investigate new places and attempt new things will take advantage of sentiments of self-development, lifting their degree of duty.

3. Maintain a strategic distance from Opportunity. In one review, therapists at the University of Vermont asked 349 people in submitted connections about sexual dreams. Completely 98 percent of the men and 80 percent of the ladies announced having envisioned a sexual experience with somebody other than their accomplice in any event

once in the past two months. The more extended couples were as one, the almost certain the two accomplices were to report such dreams.

Be that as it may, there is a major difference between fantasizing about treachery and really finishing. The most grounded hazard factor for disloyalty, analysts have discovered, exists not inside the marriage yet outside: circumstance.

For a considerable length of time, men have normally had the most chances to swindle on account of extended periods of time at the workplace, business travel, and authority over family funds. Be that as it may, today, the two people spend late hours at the workplace and travel on business. Furthermore, notwithstanding for ladies who remain at home, cellphones, email and texting have all the earmarks of being enabling them to frame increasingly hint connections outside of their relationships. Subsequently, your most obvious opportunity at devotion is to constrain openings that may enable you to stray. Submitted people keep away from circumstances that could prompt terrible choices - like lodging bars and late evenings with associates.

4. Picture Your Beloved. We as a whole realize that occasionally the more you attempt to oppose something - like dessert or a cigarette - the more you desire it. Relationship specialists state a similar guideline can impact an individual who sees a man or lady who is keen on them. The more you consider opposing the individual, the more enticing the person moves toward becoming. Instead of letting yourself know "Be great. Oppose," the better procedure is to begin considering the individual you

cherish, the amount they intend to you and what they add to your life. Concentrate on adoring contemplations and the delight of your family, not sexual want for your mate - the objective here is to clammy down the sex drive, not wake it up.

Chapter 3 – Habit Stacking

What is Habit Stacking?

Humanity should not act morally right only because it is to the overall advantage of society. The reason for this is because morals form an essential aspect of maintaining the identity of individuals living in a community. There is a close relationship between personal development and morality, with psychologists in the present-day considering morality to correspondingly change with personal development. The mannerisms and behaviors of individuals within society depend on their ability to act morally right.

Renowned psychologists such as Jean Piaget, Elliot Turiel and Lawrence Kohlberg state that morality develops through cognitive stages in the life of an individual. The reason for this is because the individual accesses different levels of information as they grow up, maturing and becoming more intelligent. The need to act in a moral manner, consequently, should not be for the benefit of the overall community, but for the development stages in the individual, as well. Morality in an individual keeps developing as long as they interact with others in society, and this is crucial in determining their behaviors and attitudes.

People should not just act in a moral manner just for the benefit of society because it has a significant influence on an individual's moral self-image. Members of the community always attempt to act in a moral manner because of a sense of responsibility and collectiveness. Maintaining a good moral self-image has an influence on the behavior of an individual because it either makes them confident or deprives them of it. Confidence in the self-image of an individual has an impact on the manner in which they will socialize with the rest of the community.

There is a very close relationship between morality and religion in society. People should not choose to act in a moral manner simply because it is to the overall advantage of society. Religious teachings show that morality should be the fabric of every community living in the world because good behavior brings human beings closer to God. Setting a good example from an individual sense creates awareness for all the members of the community. All religions emphasize the fact that the persona of God is that of a Holy One, and human beings should always try to replicate this as they were made in His likeness.

Religions have proven to be critical in dealing with different moral dilemmas that plague society. Hinduism, for instance, specifies that killing is wrong, but there are circumstances in life where it might be justified. Such justifications are made possible because of a wider understanding of religion, despite the fact that there is no synonymy between religion and morality. The life of every individual must be considered when making crucial decisions, and that is the reason why religions such as Hinduism recognize the individual over the entire community when necessary.

This is yet more evidence of the fact that people should not act morally right just for the sake of the benefit of the community. Their own ability to live and interact with everybody else in the world will depend on their ability to develop moral behaviors. Religious and morality value systems only co-exist because the principles offer a reflection of the manner in which humanity should conduct their lives. Contemporary secular frameworks such as humanism and free thought also exhibit signs of synonymy with religion. The reason for this is because they emphasize that society can only progress through the faith and contribution of each individual.

People should also not just consider acting morally just for the overall benefit of society because human progress and freedom depend on it. Several people in the world desire to truly be free from any system that weighs down their lives, but the definition of freedom is sometimes confusing. According to the philosopher Immanuel Kant, human beings are rational and therefore capable of true freedom. When people act freely, they are performing a duty in society because there is no inclination to their actions. This means that acting in a moral manner helps an individual develop their own understanding of the world without directly benefiting the overall community.

Moral actions provide a sense of duty in individuals that provides extra motivation towards being responsible. Morality makes people work in a coordinated manner, and this always offers the hope of a bright future. Acting in a moral manner is of benefit to an individual because it helps to create a sense of purpose in life through togetherness with other people. The experience of life becomes much more exciting and tolerable when acting in a moral manner because it becomes easier to socialize and interact with other people.

Moral actions help to inspire collective progress and evolution in individuals. Change is the one constant in the world that determines how societies form and survive through times. The direct consequence is that people can only achieve true personal progress by acting in a moral manner because it brings everybody together. Civilizations and modern societies would not have been able to form through history if there was not a sense of morality in human societies. The reason for this is because acting in a moral manner provides an individual with insight into the necessity of working together to get through life.

People should not act morally only because it is to the overall advantage of society as true happiness is determined by moral actions. Psychologists suggest that moral acts such as kindness and faithfulness create a sense of peace and belonging in individuals. True happiness in life can only be achieved through love, and this inspires an individual into moral actions. Moral actions offer a sense of purpose and duty, and this sense of responsibility provides genuine happiness in the life of an individual. The direct benefit for the community is obvious because such individuals are able to interact very well with the community, but performing moral actions also provides a sense of exhilaration about living life.

I believe that I have good moral character because my idea of integrity is based on kindness, mutual respect, and love. A person of high integrity, according to me, is one who is ready to help others out and display a high level of kindness even though they are not getting rewarded for their efforts. Similarly, an individual who can respect not only the people around them, but the natural environment, as well, then such an individual is worthy of high integrity according to me.

The virtues that I practice are temperance and justice because I believe that we should treat ourselves as well as others in a respectful manner. I believe that affirming the status of justice in society is important, and this results in the temperance among the population that is good for productivity. The virtues that I aspire to practice are courage and prudence; courage refers to the inner bravery to take up difficult challenges without quitting. Prudence refers to the act of being cautious, and this reflects on my renewed interest to always research and seek knowledge before making decisions.

The ethical theory that I try to follow is Kant's Ethics Theory that emphasizes moral actions are characterized by whether they fulfill the individual's responsibilities/duty. According to the theory, the decision between right and wrong is determined by whether the specific action fulfilled a pre-determined duty. Therefore, the overall consequence of the action does not determine whether it is right or wrong, and being good is determined by moral law that applies to everybody regardless of their interests. Therefore, this ethical theory emphasizes the need to treat everybody equally in society as a measure of being good and morally upstanding in society.

I believe that ethics plays a very important role in my life because it would not be possible for me to be happy without trying to be ethical. Ethics is not just about the individual, but it is about their interactions with the rest of the community and how they contribute towards general progress. Being ethical means that the individual is productive because they are able to contribute respectfully and happily towards the development and advancement of the community. I know that I would be unhappy if I tried living without trying to be ethical because everybody else would also be treating me badly.

I value ethics in my life also because it allows me to grow as an individual morally and spiritually. When an individual behaves in an ethical manner, they are able to learn more about their community and interact with an increasing number of people. By being ethical, I am able to achieve my objectives with ease because I can interact with different people as well as institutions with success. Being ethical is directly responsible for me progressing my understanding of society and how best to contribute to the advancements.

Ethics has provided me with a set of moral codes from which offer suitable guidance for every action I take. As a result of my understanding and value for ethics, I am able to conduct different activities and manage my behavior in a respectful manner. An ethical approach to life has allowed me to develop my character and respect for other people in society. I am able to make friends from all spheres of life, and I attribute this to valuing ethics highly in my life as it plays an increasingly important role in influencing my life now and in the future.

How to Apply Habit Stacking to Your Life

Habits are a ground-breaking approach to make positive changes in your life. The test is including new habits and bringing an end to unfortunate propensities.

Be that as it may, you can stack the habit deck to support you. All the more unequivocally, you can structure yourself for progress by stacking habits, or habit stacking. Habit stacking is just connecting together a chain of little activities into a daily schedule, where the entirety of the entire is more than the parts.

Build up the Habit of Following the Routine

The way to habit stacking is to manufacture the habit of playing out everyday practice. The routine should consolidate the habits into a straightforward stream that you can perform. Reiteration will enable you to fabricate the habits. Generally, it is about recurrence and stream.

The way to habit stacking is to adhere to the daily schedule rather than individual habits. You need to naturally spill out of one activity directly into the following activity without pondering every individual part. That is the reason it is imperative to build up the habit of following the daily schedule.

When you are ready to play out the habits without breaks or faltering, that is the point at which you realize you have manufactured an amazing habit stacking custom.

Here are the 8 stages for structure a habit stacking schedule;

1. **Pick a Time and Location.**
   Construct a daily schedule around a specific area, time of day or a mix of both.

2. **Construct One Routine at once.**
   Concentrate on each daily schedule in turn since it decreases the measure of consumption of your resolve. It is suggested that you center around one new daily practice for a month before rolling out any improvements or increments.

3. **Start with "Little Wins".**
   Look crosswise over territories in your life where little successes would pay you back. The 7 classes of habits are:

   - Connections
   - Recreation.
   - Association
   - Profitability
   - Funds
   - Wellbeing/physical wellness
   - Otherworldliness/prosperity

4. **Make a Logical Checklist.**
   Make a basic agenda of your habits and activities required to achieve each habit. It is suggested that the habits should cooperate and stream flawlessly. It is likewise suggested that your agenda of habits reflect

moving starting with one room then onto the next to keep the advancement streaming.

5. **Have a "Motivation behind why".**

Have a valid justification for why behind every individual activity with the goal that you don't stop. A few people receive habit stacking procedures to enable them to live more, while others embrace them to invest more energy with their families.

6. **Be Accountable.**

It is constantly simpler to do nothing than to make a move. Refreshing individuals on our advancement to enable you to stay with it. For instance, Scott attempted a scale that tweets his weight.

Be that as it may, another approach to remain responsible is to structure it. Having a caution on your telephone to trigger you to begin to utilize your schedule every day. Attempt the Lift App on the grounds that that functions admirably.

7. **Make Small, Enjoyable Rewards.**

Reward yourself with little treats for overcoming your schedule each day for a week or month. It is prescribed that you keep the reward little and pick compensates that have a positive long haul sway, for example, a motion picture, night out, or little solid treat.

8. **Concentrate on Repetition.**

Redundancy of routine helps assemble your muscle memory. Redundancy is key for the initial 30 days of habit stacking.

Case of a Productivity Habit Stacking Routine

Set my Commodore for the main assignment. (Reason: I like to work in little squares of time.

Audit my quarterly objectives. (Reason: Reviewing three-month objectives once a day encourages me to remain concentrated on my most significant ventures.)

As should be obvious, Scott fortifies taking little activities, spilling out of one habit to the following, and having a motivation behind why so he realizes both what he's attempting to achieve and why he's doing it.

Identify my three most significant undertakings. (Reason: While I have a long venture rundown of everything that should be finished during the week, I like to concentrate on achieving a couple of real 'wins' for every day.)

Guide out the activity steps and specific achievements for each undertaking. (Reason: I should be exact with the most significant errands. Rather than recording an unclear explanation, for example, 'take a shot at next book,' I record the specific outcomes I'd like to accomplish.)

Start on the most upsetting errand. (Reason: As we've examined, when you center around the hardest undertaking first, the remainder of the day doesn't appear that hard. For me, that underlying errand consistently includes some type of composing.)

Research the main 100 free and paid books in the Kindle showcase. (Reason: From a business point of view, it is imperative to monitor what's as of now selling in my market.)

Specifically, I write in 25-to 50-minute squares, utilizing a modified adaptation of the Commodore Techniques. This is one more way I can remain concentrated on the job that needs to be done.)

Clear my work area. (Reason: I like to begin working with a sorted out work area. At last that encourages me to remain concentrated on specific undertakings and not get diverted.)

Managing Habit Stacking Disruptions and Challenges

Mishaps, slipups, diversions, and interruptions will occur. The inquiry is, what will you do about it? In any case, a superior inquiry is, in what manner will rapidly refocus when you have to?

You have to realize both how to manage interruptions and how to refocus.

There are a couple of key procedures to enable you to manage interruptions and to refocus:

Procedure 1: Reduce Overall Expectations. An excessive amount of weight on yourself can cause a negative response. Rather, center on the base, however, centers around the habits that are generally significant.

Procedure 2: Have an If-Then Plan. Interruptions occur. Your responsibility is to make an arrangement for when those triggers happen. Acknowledge that interruptions occur and don't get debilitated. He additionally says to rapidly excuse yourself and proceed onward so you can refocus.

Procedure 3: Start Small (Again). Beginning once again can be disheartening, however, that is the stuff to succeed. Searching for little successes and focus on adhering to your daily practice as opposed to concentrating on the length of the daily practice. You can include more habits after you have a firm handle on your daily schedule.

Procedure 4: Know Your Triggers. To make an If-Then Plan you have to know your triggers. Your triggers are the diversions and unfortunate propensities that take you off track or where you goof. Monitoring your negative habits to enable you to build up your daily practice.

The Benefits of Habit Stacking

Exercise, reflection, feast preparing, journaling, and perusing. What do these things share practically speaking? They are little habits that I've embraced to enable me to be progressively beneficial, vivacious, and spurred.

My mornings incorporate time for reflection, smart dieting, and care, yet it wasn't constantly similar to this.

Everything began when I chose to practice before anything else. This implied I needed to turn into a morning individual.

Following a little while, practicing in the first part of the day turned into a habit that set the foundation for different habits: I began settling on better decisions about my nourishment, I started supper preparing, started drinking more water.

I stacked one habit after another.

What Is Habit-Stacking?

Habit-stacking means building one habit and stacking another habit on top. The new habit can be digressively related, or it very well may be a totally different habit that you need to create. The thought is that you start little and stack one habit after another.

Adjusting YOUR ROUTINE:

Organizing your morning schedule helps set the pace for the remainder of the day: It enables you to get into the correct mentality, gather speed toward a superior day, and improves your general personal satisfaction. Research demonstrates that morning individuals are increasingly proactive in their lives. As indicated by the Journal of Applied Social Psychology, individuals who will, in general, get up right on time around a similar time on weekdays and ends of the week have a more prominent "capacity to make a move to change a circumstance to further one's potential benefit."

How Habit-Stacking Works

1. Identify a habit you need to create and be specific about your activity:
    With regards to building up a habit, abstain from being dubious about what you are wanting to achieve. For instance, rather than saying, "I need to peruse a book each month," record your habit in an increasingly solid manner, "I need to peruse for 20 minutes every day." Or "I need to peruse for an hour on Sunday morning." You may have an objective as a primary concern, yet making it a habit can enable you to reach, or even outperform your objective, and empower you to keep that habit over a more extended timeframe.

2. Locate the ideal time to finish the habit:

    Set yourself up for progress and locate a sensible time in your day to fuse your habit. For instance, I appreciate getting up ahead of schedule to work out, however, I likewise realize that a 5 a.m. boot camp session is a lot for me. I don't feel as fiery and conscious to drive my body during a time session around then, it likewise implies I need to wake up around 4:30 a.m. to get that going. Rather, I adhere to a 6 a.m. session since I'm bound to be conscious during that time, increasingly slanted to expand my activity and complete it.

3. Create and track your habit progress:

    Building up another habit requires some investment. Here are a couple of things you can do to remain responsible, roused, and positive while attempting to set up another habit.

    Applications: Try utilizing some habit-improvement and following applications, for example, Productive, Today, or Done. These applications help you see your improvement over the long haul, empower you to build up a streak, and make you feel cheerful after you complete a habit.

    Schedule or diary: Keeping a diary or a schedule and following how you feel are incredible approaches to consider yourself responsible and screen your advancement. Think about utilizing the Passion Planner or the Panda Planner which helps supplement and empower your habit-shaping endeavors.

Responsibility accomplice: Identify a responsibility accomplice, either face to face, by telephone or gathering content. Set up a week by week call or meet with a companion to check in and keep tabs on your development or build up a gathering content with individuals who can keep you persuaded and help you recollect why you began.

4. When another habit is shaped, identify new habit:

A cornerstone habit is a habit that triggers other great habits. For instance, practicing is a cornerstone habit that can cause other positive examples in your life. A cornerstone habit triggers across the board change.

For example, specialists state families who eat together appear to bring up kids with better schoolwork aptitudes, higher evaluations, show more prominent passionate control, and display more certainty. The thought is that one little habit can stream down into other great habits. Practicing each day could enable you to feel less focused on, progressively vivacious, and help you eat better.

My Habit-Stacking in Effect

My morning habits have a specific reason or importance: they make me feel upbeat, give me an uplifting viewpoint in life, and set me up for progress. This is only a little depiction of how I've habit-stacked my morning.

One of my preferred things in my morning habits includes journaling or composing since I get the chance to record my aims and objectives for the afternoon.

Habit-Stacking Success Tips

There are a couple of things you can do to help with your habit advancement.

Take a stab at consistency: One awful feast doesn't make you undesirable, much the same as one plate of mixed greens doesn't make you a sound individual. It is your main event after some time that issues. If you don't do your habit one day, don't be so difficult on yourself and recollect that consistency is what's most significant in the whole deal.

Maintain a strategic distance from self-harm: You have been doing extraordinary with practicing and making sound sustenance alternatives. Try not to disrupt your endeavors by eating five cuts of pizza, a sack of chips, and a bundle of treats. Gradual advances is the way to progress when framing a habit. Start little so you don't set yourself up for disappointment.

Start now: You need to begin working out? Start fabricating your habit when you state you need to do it. Go get the running shoes, practice garments, and schedule or applications to keep you responsible and keep tabs on your development.

Approaches to Habit-Stack Your Morning

Your morning as of now comprises of habits, for example, making your bed or perusing the news. Here are some little approaches to habit stack your morning.

- Rest: Go to bed at a sensible hour and wake up simultaneously consistently without hitting the rest catch.
- Objectives: Write down three undertakings that you would like to achieve every day.

- Wellness: Exercise for at any rate of 30 minutes every day.
- Sustenance: Eat a nutritious breakfast.

These habits can help guarantee you are well-refreshed, stimulated, less pushed, and prepared to handle every day with the correct attitude and reason.

Chapter 4 – Self-Discipline

What is Self-Discipline?
Self-control shows up in different structures, for example, constancy, limitation, perseverance, thinking before acting, completing what you start doing, and has the capacity to do one's choices and plans, disregarding burden, hardships, or deterrents.

Self-restraint likewise implies discretion, the capacity to dodge unfortunate abundance of anything that could prompt negative results.

One of the primary attributes of self-control is the capacity to swear off moment and prompt gratification and delight, for some more noteworthy addition or all the more fulfilling outcomes, regardless of whether this requires exertion and time.

The term self-control frequently causes some distress and obstruction, because of the incorrect thought that it is something terrible, difficult to accomplish, and which requires a great deal of exertion and sacrifice. All things considered, practicing and accomplishing self-restraint can be fun, doesn't require strenuous endeavors, and the advantages are extraordinary.

Genuine self-control is definitely not a correctional or prohibitive lifestyle as certain individuals might suspect, and it has nothing to do with being extremist or living like a fakir. It is the statement of inward quality and backbone, crucial for managing the undertakings of everyday life and for the accomplishing of objectives.

Self-control, together with determination, can enable you to beat apathy, dawdling, and uncertainty. These aptitudes make it conceivable to make a move and drive forward with it, regardless of whether the activity is upsetting and requires exertion.

Self-restraint empowers you to practice balance in what you do, become progressively persistent, tolerant, understanding and kind. Likewise, it causes you to withstand outer weight and impact.

A self-taught individual is progressively dependable and puts additional time and exertion in what the individual does.

A self-trained individual is bound to assume responsibility for their life, set objectives, and find a way to accomplish them.

Self-restraint is very much depicted in the anecdote about the hare and the turtle, who directed a race between themselves.

The bunny realized that he was quicker, so he enabled himself to sleep in the race. At the same time, the turtle trudged along, yet with resolution and self-control, it in the long run figured out how to arrive first to the end goal.

Like the turtle, with self-control, you can complete what you start.

Here are a couple of statements about this significant point:

Self-restraint starts with the authority of your considerations. If you don't control what you figure, you can't control what you do. Just, self-restraint empowers you to think first and act a while later.

Order truly implies our capacity to get ourselves to do things when we don't need it.

Self-restraint is a type of opportunity. Opportunity from sluggishness and laziness, opportunity from the desires and requests of others, opportunity from shortcoming and dread and uncertainty. Self-restraint enables a pitcher to feel his distinction, his inward quality, his ability. He is ace of, instead of a captive to, his contemplations and feelings.

For quite a while, we are gone up against various choices. An abnormal state of discretion enables us to meet the choice that is most helpful over the long haul. This capacity causes us to withstand the enticement of picking the most agreeable or pleasurable choice. Deciding on the most effortless arrangement may be very appealing, yet just for a brief span. At the point when seen from a long haul viewpoint, all things considered, none of these "agreeable choices" add to your prosperity.

The peril lies in that that joy situated choices ordinarily don't in a split second negatively affect your life when taken independently. Whenever joined, be that as it may, the aggregate of all these unbeneficial small scale choices will shape your life and will, at last, decide your fate.

- The Definition of Self-Discipline
- The capacity to prepare and control one's direct.
- The capacity to do the things that should be finished.
- The capacity to control one's emotions and wants.

The thing self-control portrays the vital mental quality that is required to control one's behaviors, emotions and wants. If one is self-restrained, it demonstrates that one's emotions and wants are leveled out. It additionally demonstrates that one can rouse oneself to handle the assignments and issues that should be tended to. If you have an abnormal state of self-restraint, you will not avoid difficulties and obstructions that hinder you.

An Explanation of Self-Discipline

Self-control portrays not just the fundamental resolve required to do what should be finished. It likewise characterizes the capacity to withstand enticements so as to achieve long haul objectives. Essentially, it is your capacity to disregard everything that doesn't add to the achievement of your destinations. This incorporates contemplations, emotions, and enticements. Indeed, self-restraint encourages you to withstand the enticement of distractive exercises.

Despite the fact that we as a whole battle to be taught enough to complete disagreeable things, there are individuals who are more responsible for themselves than others. We should examine a portion of the primary driver why individuals battle to ace poise:

The Reasons for a Lack of Self-Discipline

The significant motivation behind why the vast majority battle to act naturally taught lies in a misperception of the fundamental idea. Most people misconstrue what poise really implies. These individuals partner self-restraint with something excruciating or over the top. They wish that being trained is simple and pleasurable. Consequently, at whatever point these people attempt to be progressively trained, it ends up being a battle that just feels not appropriate to them. They don't care for it by any means, which is the reason they rapidly come back to their usual range of familiarity.

Here's the significant viewpoint these people don't think about with regards to self-control:

The sole reason for the control idea is to cause you to get things done, regardless of if it is pleasurable or not.

Hence, the expectation behind self-restraint isn't to give you joy and euphoria. Its lone target is to enable you to achieve your long haul objectives. In any case, for what reason would it be advisable for you to develop something that doesn't give you happiness? The purpose behind this is basic. Every one of your endeavors and torments are remunerated once you make your fantasies materialize. Also, this is simply the genuine motivation behind why being a taught individual is so advantageous. It may not generally feel good when you compel yourself to remain trained, in any case, your reward will remunerate you.

What Is Self-Restraint?

Restraint manifests itself in a wide range of structures

This is what you can do if you are battling with self-control.

As a matter of first importance, attempt to evacuate the desire that one day you may really like being restrained. Much of the time, you will not. Be that as it may, if you are not anticipating that things should be simple, you'll be bound to proceed with the quest for being taught. Truth be told, when you anticipate that things should be difficult, you'll have the option to all the more likely manage the battles you experience.

Furthermore, it is significant that you consistently drive yourself to keep up discretion. Doing so will assist you in establishing the habit of being restrained. Not exclusively will this habit affect significant aspects of your life; however, it will likewise enable you to expand your odds to succeed.

Here are some more reasons why individuals need poise:

- Self-control isn't characteristic. It should be created, fortified, and worked out. In any case, the vast majority think that it is difficult to do as such. If you don't have the foggiest idea of how to successfully fabricate and fortify poise, it is genuinely difficult to create it in any case.

- A misinterpretation of discretion. Numerous erroneously see self-control as something that is prohibitive and difficult. They consider it to be habitual and are hesitant to reinforce it.

- Acknowledgment of disappointment can likewise add to an absence of discretion. At the point when individuals can live with the possibility of fizzling, it'll be difficult to keep up self-restraint.

- Enticements. We as a whole are faced with different sorts of allurements every day. Surrendering to these allurements takes after the section of an endless loop. If you don't have the essential resolution to withstand these enticements, it'll be considerably progressively difficult to bring an end to the negative habit.

- Absence of direction. An individual who does not have a genuine vision for life will discover it increasingly difficult to look after order. In any case, if you have a mission that you need to see acknowledged, you'll be bound to have the essential self-control to seek after it.

How about we proceed with the following point that will assist us with furthering comprehend what self-control is.

Benefits of Self-Discipline

Self-restraint Benefits

Self-restraint is one of the most significant and helpful abilities everybody ought to have. This ability is fundamental in each everyday issue, and however, the vast majority recognize its significance, not many plan something for fortifying it.

In spite of regular conviction, self-control doesn't mean being brutal toward yourself or carrying on with a constrained, prohibitive lifestyle. Self-control implies restraint, which is an indication of inward quality and control of yourself, your activities, and your responses.

Self-control enables you to adhere to your choices and finish them, without altering your perspective and is in this way, one of the significant necessities for accomplishing objectives.

The ownership of this ability empowers you to endure with your choices and plans until you achieve them. It additionally manifests as internal quality, helping you to beat addictions, stalling, and apathy, and to finish whatever you do.

Develop Willpower and Self Discipline

Start Building Your Willpower and Self Discipline

Direction and activities for structure up resolve and self-restraint, conquering tarrying, and sluggishness, picking up conclusiveness and persistence, and assuming responsibility for your life.

Develop Your Willpower and Self-Discipline

One of its principal attributes is the capacity to dismiss moment gratification and delight, for some more noteworthy increase, which requires investing exertion and energy to get it.

Self-control is one of the significant elements of accomplishment. It conveys what needs be in an assortment of ways:

Persistence.

The capacity not to surrender, in spite of disappointment and misfortunes.

restraint.

The capacity to oppose diversions or enticements.

Attempting on and on, until you achieve what you set out to do.

Life puts difficulties and issues on the way to progress and accomplishment, and so as to transcend them, you need to act with diligence and perseverance, and this obviously, requires self-restraint.

The ownership of this aptitude prompts self-assurance and confidence, and thus, to joy and fulfillment.

Then again, the absence of self-restraint prompts disappointment, misfortune, wellbeing and connections' issues, weight, and different issues.

This expertise is likewise valuable for beating dietary problems, addictions, smoking, drinking and negative habits. You likewise need it to cause yourself to sit and consider, practice your body, grow new aptitudes, and for personal development, profound development and reflection.

As said before, the vast majority recognize the significance and advantages of self-control, yet not many find a way to create and reinforce it. In any case, you can reinforce this capacity like some other aptitude. This is done through preparing and activities, which can discover at this site.

Self-Restraint Benefits and Importance

Self-restraint encourages you:

- Keep taking a shot at a venture, even after the underlying surge of eagerness has blurred away.
- Get up promptly toward the beginning of the day.
- Think normally.
- Abstain from acting thoughtlessly and on motivation.
- Satisfy guarantees you make to yourself and to other people.
- Keep taking a shot at your eating routine, and opposing the enticement of eating swelling sustenance's.
- Conquer the habit of observing a lot of TV.
- Defeat apathy and hesitation.
- Start perusing a book, and read it to the last page.

It will be simpler for you to reinforce your self-restraint if you:

Attempt to act and carry on as indicated by the choices you make, paying little respect to sluggishness, the inclination to tarry, or the craving to surrender and stop what you are doing.

Comprehend its significance in your life.

You can fortify your self-devotion regardless of whether it is as of now frail, with the assistance of uncommon basic activities, which you can rehearse whenever or place.

Become mindful of your undisciplined behavior and its outcomes. At the point when this mindfulness builds, you will be increasingly persuaded of the need to roll out an improvement in your life.

How Self-Discipline Can Improve Your Life

No close to home achievement, accomplishment, or objective, can be acknowledged without self-control. It is uniquely the most significant credit expected to accomplish any kind of close to home magnificence, athletic brilliance, virtuosity in expressions of the human experience, or generally remarkable execution.

What Is Self-Control?

It is the capacity to control one's driving forces, feelings, wants and behavior. It is having the option to turn down quick joy and moment gratification for picking up the long haul fulfillment and satisfaction from accomplishing higher and progressively significant objectives.

To have self-restraint is to have the option to settle on the choices, take the activities, and execute your strategy paying little respect to the deterrents, inconvenience, or difficulties, that may come your direction.

Unquestionably, being disciplined doesn't mean living a constraining or a prohibitive lifestyle. Nor, doesn't mean quitting any pretense of all that you appreciate, or, to give up fun and unwinding. It means figuring out how to concentrate your brain and energies on your objectives and endure until they are practiced. It likewise means developing an outlook whereby you are led by your conscious decisions as opposed to by your feelings, negative behavior patterns, or the influence of others. Self-restraint enables you to arrive at your objectives in a sensible time span and to live an all the more precise and fulfilling life.

The Most Effective Method to Develop Self-Discipline

Start with gradual steps. No procedure happens medium-term. Similarly, as it requires some investment to manufacture muscle, so does it set aside some effort to create self-control. The more you train and fabricate it, the more grounded you become. In exercise, if you attempt to do a lot on the double, you could harm yourself and have difficulty. In like manner, approach it slowly and carefully in structure self-control. Along these lines, start by settling on the choice to go ahead and realizing the stuff to arrive.

Realize what rouses you and what your awful triggers are. You can start by finding out about yourself! At times it is difficult to ward off desires and longings, so know the regions where your opposition is low and how to maintain a strategic distance from those circumstances. If you realize you can't avoid cake, fries, or different allurements - avoid them. Try not to have them around to bait you in snapshots of shortcoming. discipline If you additionally realize that putting weight on yourself doesn't work for you, at that point set yourself up in a domain that supports the structure of self-restraint as opposed to one that subverts it. Expel the allurements and encircle yourself with relieving and empowering things, for example, inspiring mottos and pictures of what you need to accomplish.

Realize additionally what empowers and propels you. Your self-control can go here and there with your vitality levels so play vigorous music to liven you up, move around, chuckle. Train yourself to appreciate what you are doing by being invigorated. This will make it simpler to actualize attractive and fitting behaviors into your daily schedule - which is truly what self-control is about.

Make certain behaviors a daily schedule. When you have chosen what's critical to you and which objectives to take a stab at, set up a day by day schedule that will enable you to accomplish them. For instance, if you need to eat soundly or get in shape; take steps to eat a few servings of foods grown from the ground every day and exercise for at any rate thirty minutes. Make it part of your day by day schedule and part of your self-control building. In like manner, dispose of a portion of your awful, reckless habits, whatever they might be. They can place you in a negative temper and impede your self-restraint. A poor frame of mind can likewise be an unfortunate habit.

Practice discipline. Figure out how to disapprove of a portion of your emotions, motivations, and desires. Train yourself to do what you know to be correct, regardless of whether you don't want to do it. Skip dessert a few nighttimes. Utmost your TV viewing. Fight the temptation to holler at somebody who has bothered you. Stop and think before you act. Consider results. When you practice patience, it encourages you to build up the habit of monitoring different things.

Take part in games or exercises. Sports are a great method to upgrade self-control. They train you to set objectives, center your psychological and emotional energies, become physically fit, and to coexist well with others. Taking an interest in games gives a circumstance where you figure out how to buckle down and endeavor to give a valiant effort, which thus, instructs you to incorporate the equivalent points of view and disciplines into your regular day to day existence.

Figuring out how to play a melodic instrument can be another extraordinary method to rehearse self-control. The center, reiteration, and application required in figuring out how to play an instrument is significant. Accomplishing self-restraint in any one aspect of your life reinvents your brain to pick what is correct, as opposed to what is simple.

Get motivation from those you appreciate. Michael Jordan has constantly kept up that his enormity as a ballplayer came as much from his readiness to buckle down at his art, as it did his ability. It was his longing through discipline and center that made him extraordinary compared to other ballplayers. If it worked for him, it could absolutely work for all of us.

Imagine the prizes. There is nothing more gratifying than achieving your objectives. Practice the system that high achievers and top competitors do. Undertaking yourself later on. Picture your ideal result. Feel how compensating it is and the incalculable advantages you will appreciate. Remind yourself the stuff to arrive.

The Benefits

It helps manufacture self-assurance.

You achieve more and are along these lines increasingly gainful.

You can keep up a higher resilience for dissatisfaction, deterrents and negative feelings.

Enables you to get better wellbeing, better funds, and a decent hard-working attitude.

You can arrive at your most difficult objectives all the more productively.

The more disciplined you become, the simpler life gets.

If we are to be experts in our own predetermination, we should create self-control and discretion. By concentrating on long haul benefits rather than transient inconvenience, we can urge ourselves to create of self-restraint. At last, our wellbeing and satisfaction rely upon it.

Fundamentals of Self-Discipline

Commitment

It is your degree of pledge to what you are doing that will choose your degree of accomplishment in it. Unfortunately, a great many people simply stop after the 'wish' part and scarcely take the torment to focus on their fantasies. Presumably, that is the thing that stops them to be fruitful in any undertaking.

We should get this straight that there is no alternate route to progress. The best way to be effective is to take the long street and pursue your interest with a hundred percent devotion and promise to it.

Notwithstanding, the way to progress isn't simple as it sounds to be. You need to make a few responsibilities to yourself to reach there and carry on with the life you have imagined in your fantasies.

Try not to give your tasks a chance to run your life. Coming up next are the seven responsibilities that one must make to himself on his interest in progress:

#1 Commitment: Taking huge activity regular

Since you comprehend what you need to seek after in life, it is an ideal opportunity to make an activity arrangement for it. Regardless of whether your objectives are little or huge, you should be subscribed to make gigantic moves each and every day for no reason.

It begins with setting up your mind to enthusiastically pursue your fantasies or whatever you are energetic about in life. You can start by making an arrangement. All things considered, there are many arranging instruments out there to enable you to out. While making your activity arrangement, ensure you redo it according to your needs and qualities.

Try not to be excessively easygoing or excessively yearning about them. Be as reasonable as could be expected under the circumstances so you are propelled enough to make a monstrous move on them regularly for no reason.

#2 Commitment: Never surrender.

As platitude' as it might sound yet never abandoning yourself is a definitive mantra to progress. As you stroll through life, you will tumble down ordinarily. You may likewise commit errors and fizzle, and it is completely alright. Such is reality and things will occur yet never let this hamper your spirits in any capacity.

Remember that so as to succeed and turn into your best form, you must have a great deal of confidence in yourself. This unyielding soul will enable you to overcome these extreme occasions a piece effectively. Try not to surrender ever — no matter what.

#3 Commitment: Being versatile and adapting constantly

Versatility and energy to develop can take you puts in life. It is dismal to see that individuals are excessively inflexible in their musings and convictions that they dismiss any proposals or new approach given to them. It very well may be perilous for their vocation and by and large life all in all.

In the expressions of Charles Darwin, "It isn't the most grounded of the species that endure, nor the most shrewd that endures. The one is the most versatile to change."

Learn as much as you can from whosoever you need as it would be something nobody can detract from you. Learn constantly as most occasions there is more than one approach to do an equivalent thing. The minute you shed your assumptions and grasp versatility, openings will consequently introduce themselves in the most unforeseen ways.

#4 Commitment: Not doing exploitative or shameless stuff

There are two different ways to succeed: the easy way and difficult one. Going for a simple way means doing 'whatever' it takes to reach there — by snare or by hoodlum. It means taking easy routes, favors, doing dishonest things that conflict with the ethical compass. Presently, the dedication isn't to do any of the things referenced previously.

You may get allured with accomplishing something unscrupulous and get snappy outcomes. Nonetheless, such things consistently accompany a cost — that can without much of a stretch ruin everything inside a snap of a finger. Keep in mind that the voyage to progress is going to test your character alongside devotion.

#5 Commitment: Believing in yourself

You must have confidence in yourself before others start putting stock in you. Whatever is that you might want to accomplish, ensure that you have confidence in it and trust your capacities to achieve it.

The issue is that individuals will, in general, think little of the capacities that prevent them to arrive at their actual potential. Take a journal and compose your qualities, uniqueness, most prominent accomplishments, and achievements in it and read them so anyone might hear each morning. This little system can do marvels to fortify your confidence in yourself.

Ordinary, I see such huge numbers of individuals with a great deal of potential however their low confidence and absence of certainty are impeding them to progress. It is basic to acknowledge yourself and put stock in capacities to carry on with your best life.

#6 Commitment: Maintaining appropriate work-life balance

Do you realize what is the absolute most significant thing in your life? It is nothing else except for your wellbeing. Your physical and psychological wellness has a significant influence on your life as everything legitimately or in a roundabout way relies upon it.

Try not to get too expended in buckling down that you start disregarding your wellbeing. If you have worked enthusiastically for straight 40 hours, it bodes well to give your body the rest it merits. If you are taking a shot at ends of the week, take a stab at spending, in any event, a couple of hours with your precious ones and energize your batteries.

#7 Commitment: Willingness to lose some rest and saying NO

Achievement regularly goes to the individuals who are happy to take the necessary steps to be effective. You would need to work your butt off as well as might need to disapprove of a few things that don't line up with your objectives.

It may entice to go out to shop or gathering with companions on ends of the week yet chipping away at your startup or composing your next blog is what is going to have to make a real effect. If you are taking a shot at your particular employment during the day then the best way to take a shot at your fantasy is by losing some rest.

One more thing, start saying NO more regularly. It may take a great deal of mental fortitude to disapprove of companions however doing it will make your life more fruitful and more joyful than theirs.

The thing about duty is that it means remaining faithful to what you said you would do long after the disposition you said it in has left you. Presently, it is up to you might want to submit yourself and follow up on things or let them transpire.

Optimization

A caffeinated drink promotion at present airing asks, "Imagine a scenario where individuals had a battery-level symbol, as on your telephone?" as we see an arrangement of individuals dressed for the workplace, exploring a city walkway, each with their own rate level, most green, some red and running out. "You'd see a great deal of us strolling around," the voice-over proceeds, "needing a revive." The drink is then exhibited as a sort of extremely quick charging link for the body.

The promotion's trick plays not exclusively to the dream that our life power can be caught in some straightforward unidimensional measure and effectively oversaw yet in addition to the more extensive, progressively guileful thought that individuals should capacity like telephones. The desires we have for our gadgets soak our desires for other people (regardless of whether they are companions, family, administration laborers, or robots) and at last ourselves. We ought to be fit for dealing with any assignment we're enlisted for, moving flawlessly starting with one interface then onto the next, starting with one application then onto the next, for whatever length of time that required. If we can't, we have to "revive" ourselves: to locate the correct medication mix or exercise routine, or else to pass on ourselves for absolutely as long as we have to return to 100 percent. The possibility that we are something besides independent and vitality autonomous is suspended for a dream of instrumental control.

Computerized systems and assets can give the figment of availability — if anybody can get to dietary rules, for example, anybody ought to have the option to tail them. This mistaken idea creates an ethical buildup: If anybody can "do it" — be sound and alluring and alarm and arranged to gain by any chance — than to not do it is an ethical coming up short. We may perceive ailment as no-flaw yet in addition rebuff any "disappointment" to treat it as indicated by social conventions.

Self-advancement turns into a type of devotion: privatized work of moral obligation as open great. This happens as a guarantee to effectiveness, as in "if you are not enhancing your life to help your work (regardless of whether that work helps anybody other than your manager) you are dead weight" — a channel on other individuals' material and enthusiastic assets. If work is life, at that point proficient objectives are good goals as well. This predicts a condition wherein wellbeing is vague from efficiency.

This week, Rebecca O'Dwyer expounds on the proliferation of temperance applications and how these work to rethink the idea. Expelled from the setting of compulsion, moderation is recast as a wellbeing practice, similar to prevailing fashion eating less junk food, and acquired line under the talk of self-advancement. By this reasoning, one can be "calm" even while consuming medications like ayahuasca or LSD to increment imaginative potential, as "moderation" is recast as a condition of availability for work.

What's in question isn't close to home wellbeing and bliss, not to mention aggregate prosperity, but instead manager requests for yield. As Alex Beattie states, "disconnectionism recodes self-care as the upkeep of a standardizing level of profitability, with internet-based life consumes fewer calories and such filling in as plain customs of control and core interest." The "advanced detox" isn't suggested to such an extent as a method for satisfaction or commitment with life yet as an administrative procedure for keeping up beneficial core interest. The defamation of diversion works as a vindication for the business cooptation of consideration.

As social backings are being destroyed and occupations are rare and frequently inadequately paid, appearing anything short of 100 percent focused on working at whatever point starts to appear to be hazardous. To release oneself is to lose critical upper hand, which is progressively conflated with a caring good and physical unfitness. As O'Dwyer brings up, the distraction some have with the details of their utilization has a superstitious cast. Fanatical self-care is simply the flipside devastation: Both can give the hallucination of authority over life's shameful acts and unusual torments, a feeling of organization — as though we generally get what we pick and what we merit.

Turning into the superhuman adaptation of yourself through eating regimen, work out, biohacking, picking up learning, and so forth and accomplishing self-enhancement is an energizing objective. In the start of your adventure towards self-streamlining, it may very well entice the need to make plenty of changes with respect to your wellbeing, wellness, and lifestyle habits on the double and to attempt to accomplish more, so you will begin to get results quicker, yet this is conceivably the quickest method to progress toward becoming overpowered. .

How would you become superhuman and arrive at self-enhancement truly? You certainly don't end up one by workaholic behavior or propelling yourself excessively hard and at last consuming yourself out.

While attempting to turn into a definitive you, it is critical to likewise deal with your emotional wellness and to permit yourself an opportunity to rest and recuperate, so you can perform ideally and perform like a superhuman when you do work or exercise.

You can be excessively determined and excessively centered around changing your wellbeing, however doing so can really harm your wellbeing at last. Making a decent attempt to turn into a solid superhuman could be what will really wind up harming your wellbeing, basically as a result of overabundance stress and uneasiness. There is no decent method to state this, however, cortisol (the primary pressure hormone) is a bitch.

If you attempt and do everything splendidly, you could make yourself stress more, and wind up hindering the procedure and your advancement. You can push hard for about fourteen days, yet then wear out and wind up taking seven days to rest, since you simply don't have the vitality.

A portion of the reactions of raised cortisol include:

Accelerating the maturing procedure by separating collagen;

Harming the safe framework, and making you bound to end up wiped out;

Setting off the creation of insulin, which can cause fat addition and increment the danger of diabetes;

State of mind changes (particularly feeling on edge, low, or effectively aggravated);

Hypertension; and

Causing the generation of more testosterone in ladies with polycystic ovarian disorder (PCOS).

Here are a couple of tips on how you can, in any case, become the superhuman rendition of you, and improve your psychological and physical execution, and accomplish self-streamlining without harming your wellbeing or sacrificing your psychological mental soundness:

Breaking Point Your Consumption of Caffeine Sources

If you can deal with having a couple of cups of espresso daily without getting to be restless, that is fine, however, if you have excessively, it can cause you to end up unsteady or on edge. When you feel on edge, you will not actually feel like a superhuman or perform like one.

Caffeine can help improve both mental and physical execution, and three cups of espresso daily should give you enough to get the advantages (that is if you can endure caffeine). A few people, similar to me, are excessively delicate to caffeine and need to remove it for the most part. The main caffeine I expend is what is found in my day by day chocolate treat that I make with cacao.

Inhale Your Way to Becoming a Superhuman

If you begin to feel overpowered by your work or the majority of the objectives that you have set for yourself, attempt to do some breathing activities. They will enable you to quiet down and remain centered. This will help decrease overpower.

You can begin by simply taking in through your eye for a couple of forgets about and for a couple. Do this for a couple of minutes and perceive how you feel. To begin with, you can put on your main tune and inhale profoundly for the term.

Ponder Your Way to Self-Optimization

This takes the entire breathing thing to the following level. By pondering, you can diminish uneasiness, remain concentrated and quiet on your superhuman and self-improvement venture, and receive the rewards that it has for your wellbeing and cerebrum. These incorporate decreasing cortisol levels, which will help fat misfortune and diminish mind haze, just as hindering maturing.

Simply reflecting for ten minutes daily is sufficient for you to begin encountering the advantages of contemplation for self-advancement.

Emotions

Have you at any point said something out of resentment that you later lamented? Do you let dread convince you not to go out on a limb that could truly profit you? If thus, you are not the only one.

The feelings are amazing. Your state of mind decides how you cooperate with individuals, how a lot of cash you spend, how you manage difficulties, and how you invest your energy.

Overseeing your feelings will enable you to turn out to be rationally more grounded. Luckily, anybody can turn out to be better at managing their feelings. Much the same as some other ability, dealing with your feelings requires practice and devotion.

Experience Uncomfortable Emotions But Don't Stay Stuck in Them

Dealing with your feelings isn't equivalent to stifling them. Disregarding your trouble or imagining you don't feel torment will not cause those feelings to leave.

Actually, unaddressed enthusiastic injuries are probably going to deteriorate after some time. Also, there is a decent shot smothering your sentiments will make you go to undesirable adapting abilities - like nourishment or liquor.

It is essential to recognize your sentiments while likewise perceiving that your feelings don't need to control you. If you wake up on an inappropriate side of the bed, you can assume responsibility for your state of mind and turn your day around. If you are irate, you can quiet yourself down.

Here are three different ways to deal with your state of mind:

1. Reframe Your Thoughts

Your feelings influence the manner in which you see occasions. If you are feeling restless and you get an email from the supervisor that says she needs to see you immediately, you may accept that you will get terminated. If in any case, you are feeling glad when you get that equivalent email, your first idea may be that you will be advanced or praised on a vocation very much done.

Consider the passionate channel you are taking a gander at the world through. At that point, reframe your considerations to build up a progressively practical view.

If you discover yourself thinking, "This systems administration occasion will be a finished exercise in futility. Nobody is going to converse with me and I'm going to resemble an imbecile," remind yourself, "It is dependent upon me to get something out of the occasion. I'll acquaint myself with new individuals and show enthusiasm for finding out about them."

At times, the simplest method to increase a different viewpoint is to make a stride back and ask yourself, "What might I say to a companion who had this issue?" Answering that question will remove a portion of the feeling from the condition so you can think all the more normally.

If you end up dwelling on negative things, you may need to change the divert in your mind. A fast physical movement, such as taking a walk or clearing off your work area, can enable you to quit ruminating.

2. Name Your Emotions

Before you can change how you believe, you have to recognize what you are encountering at the present time. It is safe to say that you are anxious? Do you feel disillusioned? It is safe to say that you are dismal?

Remember that outrage here and there covers feelings that vibe defenseless - like disgrace or humiliation. So give close consideration to what's truly going on within you.

Put a name on your feelings. Remember you may feel an entire bundle of feelings without a moment's delay - like restless, disappointed, and eager.

Marking how you feel can take a great deal of the sting out of the feeling. It can likewise help you take cautious note of how those sentiments are probably going to influence your choices.

3. Take part in a Mood Booster

When you are feeling terrible, you are probably going to take part in exercises that keep you in from that perspective. Detaching yourself, thoughtlessly looking through your telephone, or griping to individuals around you are only a couple of the ordinary "go-to terrible state of mind behaviors" you may enjoy.

In any case, those things will keep you stuck. You need to make a positive move if you need to feel much improved.

Think about the things you do when you feel cheerful. Do those things when you are feeling awful and you'll begin to feel good.

Here are a couple of instances of state of mind sponsors:

- Call a companion to discuss something charming (not to keep whining).
- Take a walk.
- Think for a couple of minutes.
- Tune in to uplifting music.

Continue Practicing Your Emotional Regulation Skills

Dealing with your feelings is intense now and again. What's more, there will probably be a specific feeling - like resentment - that occasionally bamboozles you.

Be that as it may, the additional time and consideration you spend on controlling your feelings, the rationally more grounded you'll turn into. You'll pick up trust in your capacity to deal with uneasiness while additionally realizing that you can settle on sound decisions that shift your state of mind.

Feelings are the most present, squeezing and in some cases excruciating power in our lives. We are driven step by step by our feelings. We take risks since we're energized for new prospects. We cry since we've been harmed and we make sacrifices since we cherish. No ifs, ands or buts, our feelings manage our musings, expectations, and activities with better authority than our balanced personalities. In any case, when we follow up on our feelings too rapidly, or we follow up on an inappropriate sort of feeling, we regularly settle on choices that we later regret.

Our emotions can modify hazardous limits. Veer excessively far to one side and you are verging on fury. Steer a lot to one side and you are in a condition of happiness. Similarly, as with numerous different parts of life, feelings are best met with a feeling of balance and a coherent point of view. It is not necessarily the case that we should prevent ourselves from experiencing passionate feelings for or bouncing for euphoria after extraordinary news. These really are the better things in life. It is negative feelings that must be dealt with outrageous consideration.

Negative feelings, similar to wrath, jealousy or harshness, will in general winding wild, particularly following they have been activated. In time, these sorts of feelings can develop like weeds, gradually molding the brain to work on inconvenient sentiments and ruling everyday life. Ever met an individual who's reliably irate or unfriendly? They weren't brought into the world that way. In any case, they enabled certain feelings to mix inside them for such a long time that they wound up innate sentiments emerging very every now and again.

Exercises to Improve Your Self-Discipline

What are some every day great activities to rehearse self-control?

1. **Scrub Down Every Morning**

    Cold showers suck. Driving yourself to persevere through the frigid impact of a virus shower before anything else requires discipline and a high edge for agony.

    They are difficult, they are awful, and they are not happy regardless of whether it is only for 30 seconds. Start your three day weekend by constraining yourself to persevere through intense pressure and conquer the craving for a warm and simple shower. It will be hard. In any case, it will manufacture orders like nothing else.

2. **Reflect for 10 Minutes per Day**

    Reflection may appear to be an odd method to construct discipline. All things considered, you simply need to sit on your butt and consider nothing, isn't that so? All things considered, not actually. Reflection expects you to teach your musings. To clear your brain, focus your body, and reconnect with your breath.

    Contemplation causes you to get out of the psychological mess and enables you to reconnect with yourself. What's more, it is harder than you might suspect. Sitting and pondering only your breath requires gigantic control and core interest. If you are happy to give this a go for 30 days, you will build your control and self-discipline in astonishing ways.

3. Start Your Day With 100 Push-Ups or a 1-Mile Run

100 push-ups should just take you 5 minutes. A one-mile run takes around 10 minutes. Be that as it may, they are amazing assets for structure discipline. By beginning your day with some type of physical activity, you will kick off your prosperity for the duration of the day and power yourself to accomplish something awkward and difficult before anything else.

Do this before your morning cold shower and you will have indicated more order before 8 a.m. than the vast majority do ALL day.

4. Make Your Bed

Making your bed takes 5 minutes. However, it is a little movement that requires discipline in light of the fact that there is no genuine motivation to do it. Certainly, it enables you to achieve one errand before you kick your three day weekend.

Be that as it may, dislike making your bed will expand your salary, make you progressively beneficial, or increment your sex advance. It is a definitive pointless activity. Be that as it may, you should, in any case, do it. Making your bed before anything else places you into a taught and profitable state promptly when you start your day.

It is likewise an amazing inspiration to remain wakeful as opposed to slithering into the warm sheets.

5. Dispense with Distractions

Diversions murder discipline. If you need to be increasingly trained for the duration of the day, kill all diversions. Mood killer your telephone, introduce a Facebook news channel blocker, turn off notifications on your PC and spotlight just on the job that needs to be done.

This will enable you to be progressively engaged and gainful and will require enormous measures of everyday discipline. Staying away from the dopamine-instigating internet based life notifications and instant messages isn't simple, however, it is well justified, despite all the trouble.

6. Stop Complaining

Grumbling resembles malignant growth in your spirit. You have a great deal to be appreciative for. However, every time you gripe, you disclose to yourself that your life sucks and that things are not the manner in which that they ought to be (notwithstanding when they are incredible).

So quit grumbling.

It resembles a toxin. It occupies you from the great and makes you center around everything that isn't right. It makes other individuals like you less, makes you pass up on chances, and diverts you from carrying on with an astonishing life.

Purchase an elastic band and put it on your correct wrist. If you end up whining for the duration of the day, move it to one side wrist. You will likely make it 30 days with that elastic band remaining on your correct hand. If you can do this, your control, satisfaction, and inspiration will soar.

Self-control and Willpower - Your Inner Strength

These two abilities are the providers of inward quality. They can enable you to transform you and change your habits. They are the most helpful abilities for everybody, in each everyday issue and for any age.

Self-restraint and resolution invigorate the internal to act, get things done, and to proceed with your activities, regardless of difficulties and impediments.

The total manual for resolve and self-control

Ask yourself the accompanying inquiries:

How frequently have you attempted to change your dietary patterns, quit smoking, or rise prior to the beginning of the day, yet you didn't have enough inward quality and ingenuity?

Do you some of the time, feel that you come up short on the internal solidarity to make a move, demonstration decisively or drive forward?

How often you have you chosen to take a walk, realizing how brilliant you feel a while later, however because of lethargy or absence of inward quality, you remained at home and stared at the TV?

Do you start getting things done, however, quit after a brief time?

Are there any habits that you need to change, however, feel that you come up short on the fundamental internal solidarity to change?

You can change this behavior when you reinforce your self-restraint and resolution. All you need is some preparation, direction, and counsel.

Subsequent to creating and reinforcing your resolve and create self-control, you will have the option to pick your responses and beat negative habits. These two abilities make you feel all the more dominant, sure, and responsible for yourself and of your life.

There is a misinterpretation in the open personality in regards to the two aptitudes we are discussing here. It is incorrectly accepted that their advancement requires a ton of mental and physical strain and exertion. This isn't valid. You can develop these abilities through basic activities, and even appreciate the procedure.

Develop Willpower and Self Discipline

Start Building Your Willpower and Self Discipline

Direction and activities for structure up resolution and self-control, conquering dawdling, and sluggishness, picking up definitiveness and tirelessness, and assuming responsibility for your life.

Develop Your Willpower and Self-Discipline

It is said that individuals with more prominent discretion are more joyful than individuals who don't have this capacity. Self-taught individuals additionally have inward quality, which causes them to bargain all the more effectively and certainly with issues and deterrents.

At the point when these two aptitudes are well-created, there is more control, more power, and more confidence, and one stands behind their choices. This implies better odds of achieving what one sets to do.

Self-restrained individuals ordinarily have more determination than others and don't enable their decisions to be directed by motivations or emotions and what other individuals state or do.

Conclusion

Thank you for making it through to the end of *Learn Habits of Highly Effective People & How to Increase Self Discipline*, let's hope it was informative and able to provide you with all of the tools you need to achieve your goals whatever they may be.

The next step is to like us on social media and put to practice what you learn from here.

Secrets of Stoicism

Discover the Stoic Philosophy and the Art of Happiness; Increase Your Emotions and Everyday Modern Life by Following This Beginners Guide Suited for Entrepreneurs!

Pamela Hughes

Introduction

Many thanks for choosing us to share our knowledge with you on Stoicism. If Stoicism were a tree, we would cut it down, use its roots and leaves to make medicine, its branches to make beautiful benches to sit on while we enjoy its fruits. Thank God it is not, lest we be accused of deforestation but all the same we promise to share this "tree" with you. The goal of this book is to leave you with an underlying knowledge of Stoicism, how it helped people in ancient times, and how it can help you in today's world.

In this book, we will cover the following:
- The history of Stoicism
- The backgrounds of Stoicism
- The first two topos; logic and physics
- The third topos; ethics
- Apatheia and the stoic treatment of emotions
- Stoics after the Hellenistic era
- Contemporary Stoicism

Stoicism is a way of life that inclined people to act modestly and be of good character. As a reward, they were blessed with not only fortune and wealth but also happiness. With that said, I am hoping that by the time you complete this book, you will have decided on whether Stoicism is the right way of life or not. This book should open your eyes to whether Stoicism is a sham, or it is a philosophy that still works in modern society. Tighten your seat belts as we are about to embark on a long 'statistic journey' as we are not planning on leaving any stone unturned.

Chapter 1: History of Stoicism

Stoicism is a philosophy that enables people to exist in the best possible manner. It is used to help people lessen negative emotions, increase the positive ones, and help them polish their intrinsic worth. Stoicism provides practical ways to harvest more only from what was necessary. Stoicism is not complicated, and in its simplicity, it paves the way for practical ways to find serenity and advance a person's positive attributes.

Stoicism comes from prehistoric Greece and Rome at the beginning of the 3rd century B.C. Back then, people thought differently from the people of today. Their primary concern was avoiding poverty, and this made them behave, think, and make decisions geared towards preventing that. It is of great essence to note that they were aware that avoiding poverty was not a ticket to happiness. Despite their primary goal being to avoid poverty, they also aimed at an understanding of ways to have a brilliant soul. Stoicism became famous because it gave answers to fear, anxiety, and stress. It also provided solutions to day to day trials.

This philosophy encouraged good behaviors to get better life experiences. People worked towards having good behaviors for a reward of a better life and avoid negative behavior as the pay for that was a challenging life with problems. In summary, Stoicism was an ancient way of life that taught people how to live in a particular way. It focused on having good behaviors to reduce negativity and increase contentment. This philosophy has been tried and tested by famous philosophers like Tom Brady, Thomas Jefferson, George Washington, and many others. Stoicism might have started a long time ago, but it is as relevant today as it was then. What was the goal of Stoicism? It was created to be simple to understand, easy to act on it and be useful in our lives.

The stoics were a group of philosophers who formed the Stoic philosophy. Let us look at some of the stoics that contributed to this great philosophy.

- **Marcus Aurelius**

Now, Marcus was one remarkable and most influential person in the history of human beings. For two decades, he was the head of the Roman Empire. It was during his reign that Rome was the most civilized part of the world. Did I mention that he was a remarkable human being? Of course, history has recorded overtime on how Marcus never abused his power but instead lived the Stoic way of life. His writings on how he struggled to live as an honorable human being were discovered and published as Meditations. His writings made him the best example of how Stoicism helps people to deal with day to day stresses. Marcus Aurelius lived the stoic life as one good and wise human being.

- **Lucius Annaeus Seneca**

Lucius was a dramatist, writer, and statesman. His careers gave him a good grasp of words and real charisma. He explained Stoicism and memorably. His writings are the best start for anybody to begin the journey of philosophy. His thoughts easily resonate with the modern world of today because of the practical examples given on altruism, friendship, mortality, and time management.

Chapter 2: Background of Stoicism

Today's scholars only recognize three phases of Stoicism the early Stoa, the middle Stoa, and late Stoa. Of course, Stoicism was also a modification of the former schools of thought. Its influence was extensive even after the closure of philosophical schools in 529 C.E. by the Emperor of Byzantine Emperor Justinian I.

Philosophical Antecedents

Stoicism, being a Hellenistic eudaimonic, gets its influence from the former schools of thought, but at the same, it is openly critical to some of their ideology. The schools of thoughts that preceded Stoicism are:

- Aristotelianism
- Platonism
- Cynicism
- Skepticism
- Epicureanism

Eudaimonia was a word that represented happiness and flourishing. To the Greco-Romans, eudaimonia often represented good moral virtues. Stoicism stood out because of its different context from some school of thoughts of that time with the same ideology. For instance, Euthydemus, states there are only four good virtues, and everything else is neither bad nor good. According to McBrayer, the attributes are courage, temperance, justice, and wisdom. To Aristotle, the virtues were twelve, and all were important but not adequate for eudaimonia. Aristotle also explained that both effort and luck contribute significantly to a flourishing life.

The most significant contrast is seen in Cynics, where he agreed with Socrates that the only good was a virtue but disagreed with Aristotle's additions terming them as distractions. Cynics preached a simple life that is challenging to practice. They stated that virtue was the only good and that things like education, health, or wealth may or may not be preferred. Aristotelians, on the other hand, preached aristocratic, which explained that eudaimonia could not be achieved without some privileges.

Greek Stoicism

Exponents of Stoicism came from the Eastern Mediterranean. Stoicism was Socratic, and even the Stoics accepted that label. Zeno got his information from Cynic Crates, Epictetus writings, and his teachers Stilpo and Polemo. Zeno established the three topoi logic, physics, and ethics. Zeno of Tarsus and Diogenes of Babylon were the principal heads of Stoa for a long time, even though their contributions were not significant.

In 155 B.C., three heads of Athens' significant schools went to Rome for diplomatic reasons. The Roman public loved their public performances, and at the same time, they rubbed one Roman elite the wrong way, and this bore tension between politicians and philosophers. Between late II Century B.C.E. and early I Century B.C.E., Stoics renewed their liaison with the Academy. Poisonous and Panaetius sought an agreement among the Stoicism, Academicism, and Aristotelianism. This move brought Stoicism success.

Roman Stoicism

Between 88 and 86 B.C.E, Athenian, Peripatetic, and Epicurean Ariston led politics in Athens. In 92 B.C.E, Rome defeated Mithridates, and since Athens was in support of them, it was also defeated. It made philosophers escape to different places in the Mediterranean. Stoics emulated Cato the Younger because of his opposition to Julius Caesar. In the late First Century, Arius and Tarsus were the Stoic figures. In the Imperial period, the most excellent Stoics were Epictetus, Musonius Rufus, and Marcus Aurelius.

Between the Late Republic and the Empire, we get Stoicism from some sources like Cicero's books and Diogenes Laertius' literature. Some Stoics were persecuted through murder or exile during the reigns of Vespasian, Nero, and Domitian. Seneca committed suicide following Nero's orders, and Epictetus exiled. According to Gill, Epictetus was strict while Marcus was open.

Debate with other Hellenistic School

Hellenistic school of philosophy evolved because of dialogue among the philosophers. The dialogue brought about revision or adoption of new ideologies from other schools. The discussion was between Epicureanism, Platonism, Cynicism, Aristotelianism, and Epicureanism. Let us look at some examples to see how revision and adoption contributed to this evolution. Epictetus disagreed with Epicureans on their concern with pain and pleasure. For instance, Discourses 1.2.3 are all against Epicurus. Epictetus even suggests that Epicurus is confused and advises him to retire. Epictetus also attacked Skeptics by telling them that they keep proving themselves wrong every day, and they never give up. All the same, not all Stoics were against Epicurean and Academic.

Cicero hinted on the disagreement between Aristotelians and Stoics in his book De Finibus. We also have documented examples of change of Stoic's opinion because of being challenged by other schools. A good example is when Philopator adopted the determinism modified position because of criticism from Peripatetic. Stoic ideas were also included by other schools like Antiochus of Ascalon, who claimed that Zeno's ideas were embedded in Plato. We should also note that Stoicism evolved in Christianity through Middle Platonism.

Chapter 3: First Two Topoi

Logic

An essential part of Stoic philosophy is the two topics. It shows that ethic at the center and supported by physics and logic. Ethics, physics, and logic form Stoicism three topoi. Let us take a closer look at the logic as our first topoi.

There were early contributions by the Stoic on logic, and we have writings to support that. Stoics stated that their ideal figure Sage could attain faultless knowledge but relied on moral and cognitive progress in practice. It was because physics and logic are related to ethics and works in for its service. This idea was called "prokope," and it brought a dispute with Academic Skeptics. Stoics did not state that all parody was really like the Epicureans. They agreed that some were 'cataleptic' while others were not. Diogenes explained the differences better in VII.46. He stated that cataleptic comes from something existing while non-cataleptic comes from not living.

Stoics agreed that someone could have a wrong perception either in the form of a dream or hallucinations but at the same time, stated that with proper training, someone could distinguish cataleptic from non-cataleptic. Chrysippus said that impressions are essential to absorb because by doing so, we accumulate ideas that help us to form concepts and to make progress. We should note that cataleptic is not moderate knowledge. The Stoics impression was among apprehension, opinion, and education. An ascent of a cataleptic impact brings experience. Stoics supported a justification view and hence, one theory of truth like O'Connor.

Hankinson commented on the Academic Skeptics and Stoics dispute. Here, we find Stoic growth because of external pressure. Cicero lets us know that Zeno knew that an impression could come out of something existing and non-existing. It might not have solved the dispute, but it enhanced Stoic's growth on its impression that there can never exist two or more things that are precisely similar. Frede also brought growth to this view that the cataleptic impression becomes clear not because of any internal feature but because of the external elements. According to Frede, then Stoic is more "externalist" than "internalist." Skeptics' criticism showed evidence that they relied on knowledge (Goldman 94).

Athenaeus gives a story on Sphaerus, who was a student and colleague to Cleanthes and Chrysippus, respectively. He was shown a banquet of wax birds and was accused of giving assent to fake impressions when he tried to pick one. Sphaerus was clever, and he replied that he gave permission to the proposition of the thought of them being real but not to the actual claim that they were real birds. Stoic logic distinguished between "assertibles" and "sayables." "Sayables" are imperatives, questions oaths, curses, invocations, and also include "assertible." "Assertibles," on the other hand, are "sayables" that help us to make statements. The difference between Fregean propositions and Stoic's "assertibles" is that time can bring change to the truth or deception of "assertibles." Stoic's concerns were on their argument's validity and not on logic and truth. They also used logic to guard ethics and introduced modality to that logic.

Physics

This topoi encompasses metaphysics, theology, and the natural science of today's world. We will take a look at each one of them individually.

When it comes to metaphysically, they were determinists. According to Cicero, even if circumstances surrounding two events are similar, it is not a must that the results are similar, but they can be in the future even with the same factors to consider. Stoics did not include a chance in their concept, but that does not mean they did not think of it. No, they found it as a determinant of ignorance, and just like in today's world, events are simply events, and we don't know their causes. In theology, Stoics believed that there were living and non-living things. They recognized living things, including soul and God, and non-living things like void and time. It might contradict their stand on materialism, but to be fair, it is almost similar to modern philosophists who agree that one can talk of the abstract concept because we are the only ones who can judge ourselves physically.

They sought to understand nature through two principles; active and passive principles: logos, the active one, and the passive one that consists of substance and matter. The active principle cannot be generated and cannot be destroyed while the passive principle in the form of air, water, fire, and earth can be destroyed and created again. According to Stoics, cosmic conflagrations replicate themselves the same way because of nature and cannot change. It shows that the Stoics were not aware of God out of time and space because they reasoned that something spiritual could not take action on things, because it has no underlying powers. From all of that, White explains that it brings about a biological instead of a mechanical picture of the cause. It is considerably different from philosophies after Cartesian and Newtonian philosophy.

Some modern models also show varied or identical universe but do away with providence. Eusebius was quoted by White, stating that fire is like a seed that holds the principle of all substances causes of past, present, and future occurrences. Cicero explains the Stoic theory in De Fato by equating fate to the predecessor causes. Chrypissus also argued that there is never a movement without reason and relates that there is a cause for everything. This concept made Stoics embrace divination, not a false notion but as a subdivision of physic. Stoics accepted that for a person to predict the future, you don't ignore the laws, but you exploit them.

For cosmology and natural science, human beings should understand nature and allow it to assist us in having a eudaimonic life. For fundamental ontology, Stoics explained that atoms debased the concept of their seamless unity. The effects of physics on ethics are apparent, and Cicero summarizes them when he says that Chrysippus focused on the middle position in what we can view as a position between libertarianism and in compatibilism in the modern world. White and Spinoza took the weight away from honorable responsibility to dignity and self-worth.

Chapter 4: The Third Topos (Ethics)

This third topoi was a practical one. Ethics being the study of how people live their lives, was not easy. Early Stoics had a theoretical approach. Cleanthes, Zeno, and Chrysippus systematized and defended their doctrines from critics from Academics skeptics and Epicureans. They conceived the human nature as a social animal that would bring justice to people in regards to the way they lived — oikeiosis, which was a Stoic concept also related to this idea. For stoics, human beings have instincts that can be significantly advanced as we grow from childhood to adulthood — Stoics associated these instincts to justice, courage, temperance, and practical wisdom. We pursue goals using courage and temperance, justice is an extension for the concern on the increase of people in the world, and practical wisdom gives us knowledge on how to handle what we encounter in life.

Stoics accepted the four virtues and added more in each category. A good example is practical wisdom also included discretion and good judgment. Temperance carried self-honor, dignity, and self-control. Courage consisted of confidence, perseverance, and magnanimity. Justice, on the other hand, was associated with piety, sociability, and kindness. Chrysippus also explained the pluralism idea, and this unified the virtues more and made them inseparable. Haddot drew a different parallel between the virtues, the topois and Stoic discipline, which consist of action, assent, and desire. Desire or Stoic acceptance consists of teaching yourself to accept only the things found in the universe and nothing beyond that. Work, which is Stoic philanthropy, consists of human beings who should train themselves to be concerned by others in exercising justice. The discipline of assent, also known as Stoic mindfulness consists of human beings should know how to make decisions on what to reject and accept in this life by making a proper judgment.

Ethics tries to balance between elitists' view and asceticism. It elaborated on Stoics' view on dispreferred and preferred, as explained in the book on ethics by Zeno. Zeno taught the difference in things with value and without value. The first group consisted of health, education, and wealth, while the second one consisted of poverty, sickness, and ignorance. This move was a good one, and it enabled them to harvest from both the Peripatetic and Cynics. The connection between ethics and physics is that studying physics influences our understanding of ethics. Gregory Vlatos argued that 'theocratic' affects our concept of the relation between the order of cosmos and virtue. It is brought about by physics informing ethics through underdetermined fashion. Ethics is also not free from physics, as it can be understood directly through it. Many Stoics support Vlatos position, but some do not have a clear stand on the matter.

On the same ground, it would be fair to state that ancient stoic believed there was a god that was represented by the rational principle that arranged the cosmos and that distributed throughout the world in a manner that can be described as Pantheistic. We can also argue that Stoic metaphysics leave room for Atom or God, which they developed after being criticized by Epicureans.

Chapter 5: Apatheia and the Stoic Treatment of Emotions

In this chapter, we will focus on the differences between the Epicureans and Stoics. Epicureans' points out the different places that Stoas differs from Garden; he tells Lucilius, who is his friend, that he has no problem in borrowing ideologies from Epicurus as long as he sees sense in it. He tells him that he crosses the border as a spy and not as a deserter. As we had stated earlier, Stoics thought that the essential thing in this life is virtue, while Epicureans felt that it was to live moderately and avoid pain. All the same, eudaimonia was something that both schools upheld, and it was similar to both. To Stoics, it was apatheia, while to Epicureans, it was ataraxia. It was, however, evident that there were some differences in the two concepts, especially in how people would achieve the different states.

According to Epictetus, apatheia is liberty from passion, and ataraxia is tranquility. It is good to elaborate that 'passion' did not mean what we know in the current world. Today passion is all about emotions, but according to Stoics, passion was divided into healthy and unhealthy. In unhealthy, it consisted of fear, pleasure, pain, craving while in unhealthy, there was a delight, willing, discretion. It is good to note that pain did not have a corresponding positive item. To Stoics, passion is not emotions and instinctive reactions but consequences of judgment and asserting something. Stoics knew that there were reactions that we cannot control and, for that reason, focused on responses that we can control.

To Stoics, pain is not the hurt we feel, but the act of not avoiding something we know is terrible. Fear is expecting something terrible to happen; craving is the act of wanting something we term as good; pleasure is the act of choosing something not worth. On the other hand, eupatheiai is brought about by avoiding bad things, a good desire for willingness, and happiness over delight. All these are the reasons apatheia equates us in our experiences from what life throws at us: if we reason in those experiences, we will not care about the things that do not warrant our concern and be happy in the things that concern us.

Another difference between the two schools of thought is the route they take to get to apatheia and ataraxia. To Epicureans, ataraxia was an achievement that was obtained by avoiding pain and keeping away from political and social life. Epicurus sought close friendships but avoided extending their interactions further to avoid experiencing physical and mental pain. Stoic had a goal of exercising virtue, and this made them social beings. Marcus Aurelius insistently stated in Meditations that we need to wake up every day in the morning to be useful in our societies. Hierocles explained further cosmopolitism concept. It told how human beings should follow nature and be social while still making rational judgments. We can conclusively say that apatheia was not a Stoic's goal but a fruit of having a virtuous life.

Chapter 6: Stoicism after the Hellenistic Era

Stoicism has had an enormous influence in the modern world on Western philosophy; As Long listed the philosophers affected by Stoicism as Kant, Adam Smith, Descartes, Thomas More, Rousseau, Leibniz, and Augustine. These philosophers are affected either directly, indirectly, or both. During the Renaissance, Seneca's letter and Enchiridion, both of which were Stoics books, leaned towards Stoicism and were read widely, e.g., De Offissis by Cicero. Christianity sympathized with Stoicism more than Epicureanism. The Epicureans choice to support pleasure and cosmic chaos could not mix with the ideologies of Christianity. Stoic support on materialism was rejected and highly criticized while they readily accepted Logos.

Christians have mixed feelings about Stoicism. Augustine wrote favoring words on it but later rejected it. Tertullian supported Stoicism and some Enchiridion. John and Peter Abelard also promoted it while Thomas was so critical of it. Justus Lipsius revived Stoicism during Renaissance. He was a classical philologist and humanist who published editions of Tacitus and Seneca. He explained that Christians could find help from Stoicism when in trouble but also pointed the ideologies in Stoicism that are unacceptable in Christianity.

NeoStoicism had a mixed reception. Calvi was critical of the "Novi stoic" even before Justus did as it wanted the revival of apatheia. Sellars notes that one NeoStoicism text started with a cautioning remark to stop the sharp criticism. NeoStoicism was not fully embraced as its impact is mostly from Justus and maybe some little influence from Montaigne. The essential philosopher of the modern world who was influenced by Stoicism is Spinoza. Leibniz accused him of being a sect leader with Descartes. There are some similarities between the Stoic understanding of the world and Spinoza's. In both of them, they have a God that controls nature and the universe. Well, Stoics indeed understand the cosmos as dual, but in contradicting Spinoza's concept, the "passive" and "active" principles of the Stoics were intertwined and produced unitary reality.

As Long shows us that the difference was in Spinoza's understanding that God has infinite attributes was contradictory to the Stoic's finite God. He also points out that the similarities are more if we think in terms of ethics. Due to this, Spinoza's ethics are the same as Stoics'. With that knowledge, we can look at another difference in that Spinoza declined to believe in a hidden teleology to this universe. He thought that there is no God and that nature didn't have an aim. To understand better, we can take Spinoza as the staircase leading to the Stoic system.

Lastly, we will look at the connection between Kant and the Stoic, especially duty, which beyond the consequences of a person's actions. It is As Long who points out the differences again, and Kant used reasoning to make his system while the Stoics were natural and pure at heart. This difference is also found in deontological systems and eudemonistic systems like Kant's and the Stoic's. It is only recently that they want to revive Stoicism as a realistic moral philosophy.

Chapter 7: Contemporary Stoicism

In today's world, we see revivals of Stoicism and ethics. Such works by some philosophers have revived virtue ethics as an alternative for deontological approaches. According to David Chalmers and David Bourget, their philosophy states that deontology is the leading framework with 26% followed closely by consequentialism with 24% and then lagging behind we find virtue ethics with a score of 18% and other positions getting less support. It is evident that ethics is not a recognition contest, but the above percentages show that the revival of virtue ethics in today's philosophy and biographies happens at a constant rate. Specifically, Stoicism works are more pronounced, and they appear at a high standard. Some examples are Inwood 2003, Brower 2014, Graver 2007, McGlynn 2009, Goodman 2012, and many more.

We can also say that Stoicism is going back to its roots as ancient Stoics upheld their systems as practical guidance for day to day life experiences and not theoretical. Epictetus did not mince his words to try and hide his contempt for theoretical philosophies. He stated that the theories taught us how to examine arguments and to attain the skills people need to assess logic, but in reality and practicality, what we say today as users might be wrong tomorrow. We can find the roots of modern Stoicism from Frankl's logotherapy and Albert Ellis. Stoicism is not a therapy but a philosophy, and some philosophers like John Sellars, Lawrence Barker, and William Irvine gave examples of 21st century Stoicism. All of these philosophers attempted to separate the philosophical denotation of "stoic" from Stoic as a common English word that shows a person who walks in this life with a stiff upper lip. Despite the differences, there are similarities in both; for instance, they both emphasize endurance.

Becker and Irvine explained well their attempts to revive Stoicism for today's modern society. Irvine contributed that some things like actions and our judgment are up to us, while others like the past and natural occurrences we have no control of. He also noted that we have partial control over several other things. To explain more about Irvine's philosophy, we can take an example of a baseball. For the results of the baseball game, we have part control; we can play well or poorly and influence the results, but some variables we have no control of like the impartiality of the referee. In such a game, your aim should not be to win but to do your best since that is what you have control over.

Becker expounded on it better. He notes that there are differences between the ancient Stoicism and the modern one. Becker and Irvine's attempts to revive Stoicism will be determined by future philosophies and the birth of popular movements. Since the early 21st century, we have seen significant growth in that movement. We have several blogs dedicated to modern Stoicism, e.g., Stoicism Today. We also have a considerable emergence of such groups in social media, e.g., Stoicism Group on Facebook.

Chapter 8: Stoics Spiritual Exercises

Practice Misfortune

It is not easy to be in the worst situation, for instance, to be the poorest person to be the ugliest person on earth. Stoics believe that it can happen that you find yourself in such misfortunes, and therefore, it is imperative to have an experience or a taste a situation with such misfortunes. For example, when you are a rich man, take a few days and assume that you are not rich but poor. Think of the kind of clothes worn by poor people, the kind of food they eat, and where they sleep, among other difficulties they experience in their state. Practice living like a poor man going through the worst experiences he goes through; do not be tempted to go back to your riches before the days you have set for the practice are over. Remember, it is not imagination; it is about doing it and practicing it.

This practice is important once in a while as it makes one not to be a slave of being in a certain condition or owning a certain property. It gives you a chance to taste both sides of life, and therefore, make you go through life without the feeling of anxiety and fear that is caused by the uncertainty of life; remember fear and anxiety only comes when you do not know about the future, it is not about the past. Practice, therefore, should be about something that you fear that could happen to you; practice using the worst-case scenarios.

Train Perception to Avoid Good and Bad

Training perception means whatever the experienced, there is always a good side of it. Stoics believe that when a person is faced with problems, he or she can overturn the bad experience or problem into an opportunity to get experience good things. One of the stoics, Epictetus, said that every man has resources within him or her that can help in coping with any challenge. For instance, when one goes through a painful experience, he or she develops endurance; a characteristic that is required may be in the future.

Sometimes we are disappointed by the turnout of events, which drains a lot of energy from our bodies; in this case, you lose and stain yourself mentally and physically. Instead of going through all these strenuous experiences, it is better to accept the situation and everything surrounding it, and exercise virtue; at least you will become better after the experience. It is not easy to accept everything that brings disappointments, but step by step accept that everything happens for you to be better, and it is only you to take the opportunity to grow and enjoy every minute of it.

Accepting the negative experience and turning it into an opportunity is all about perception. The stoic practice involves going past your first perception about a certain happening; tie it down to enable yourself to see things being the problem. For example, your mother dies when you are still a teenager, and according to you, you still needed her around because you have not yet matured enough to take care of yourself. However, beyond the loss, there is an opportunity for you to now become a mature and responsible person. Therefore, when you experience difficulties, you can always choose the best option that will help you to become a better person.

Remember – It's All Ephemeral

Stoics do not take everything they own to be more important or use their achievements to make themselves look big. Remember the close friend or family member that you loved very much, he or she was taken away from you: he or she died. Remember the prominent people in the world, the founder of Apple company, the scientists who discovered the scientific laws that are still in use today; they all died despite their achievement and prominence. This means that even with your achievements, you are very small, and your body and mind that you used to get all that is taken from you. The rich in the world also die living their properties; you cannot be tied to your possessions forever. This means that all that you have on earth are not yours, and therefore, just consider them as borrowed things. When you borrow something from a friend, you do not hold on it so much; you use it a return it to the owner. Similarly, all things on earth should be considered as borrowed, and therefore, only use them when you have them; do not hold on them or develop an attachment because, within no time, you can lose all of them.

It is, therefore, useless to feel anger for something you were denied or something that was precious to you and destroyed by another person. Do not hurt others because you are the richest man on earth, the prominent politician, or the famous football player. It is all nothing or very small, and within no time, you can lose them, and your name will only be read in books. therefore, it is important to practice that before you hurt someone or do unthinkable because of a property you love so much, remember that all is not yours, including your body, friends, and family members.

Take the View From Above

Stoics like looking at life at a wider view, which is known as looking from above. Looking from above is being at a place that is high in the sky and seeing so many things that are in your habitat, which is the earth. You can only take that view if you are out of this world, I mean, when you are dead. In that state, on the earth, you will see the animals, water in the lakes, oceans, and rivers, soils, and plantation. There is a variety of creations, but some are in extinction. Looking at the earth, one would visualize the people who have gone through the same world, those who are still alive on those who will be there in the coming years. Some you have never seen them, and yet you live with them in the same world, and the ones who will live in the coming years, you will never see them. Looking at everything you realize that there must be a role you played on the earth, was it big or was it small that it did not have an impact on the earth and all the things and non-living things. You cannot turn back times to relive the life that you lived before you died so as you make the impact that you feel is big enough to influence life on the earth. This means that when you have lived life, there is no need to dwell on what has already passed; the only thing that you can change is the life that you are living today, and therefore, only appreciate what was done in the past and appreciate it.

This exercise helps you to look at things from a wider perspective and is always used by those who aspire to live a better life than the one they lived in the past. The mistake most people do is that when they make a small mistake, they dwell on it, forgetting that they still have a life ahead of them; regrets only pull you behind, and therefore, only focus on the most important things, which can change your life. The exercise and practice that lets you look at life without making a conclusion about your own life by looking at the past; look at it on a wider perspective by first appreciating what life offers you in the present and maximize on the opportunity you have to be happy, achieve what you can within the time you are remaining with on the earth.

You can also look at life from a wider perspective by looking at the misfortune of others. You are still alive while other people are dead, you are healthy while others are fighting for their life on the life-saving machine. You are happy with your spouse; though you are poor, we have some people who live in a palatial house, and yet they know no peace. You might be looking at your life and think that yours is a miserable life, but when you look at other people, you will realize that life has given you much more than you deserve, and therefore, just appreciate and make good out of it.

Memento Mori (Meditate on Your Mortality)

Meditating on your mortality is reminding yourself that you will not live forever, and no one knows the day they would die. Therefore, each day, you should meditate about your death like now. If I were to die right now, how will I be like in terms of my deeds? This, though, makes one think about what they say and what they do in their lives. The meditation reminds you can die anytime and, therefore, do not waste any minute of your life, use it to do a good thing, and make other people happy.

Some people criticize this exercise by saying that it makes death as the end of everything, and yet it is not. However, it is not only those who are about to die that hurry to make life purposeful and full of good things. The practice is meant to remind you of ding good things every day; thus, it helps you to live the life that you desire. This is a life that is full of goodness and fulfillment.

Spent more time with the people that God has given you, do that thing that you are postponing at the moment because you are not sure of tomorrow. This exercise helps also to manage time well and make use of the chances provided to us all the time.

Is This within My Control

Our happiness is determined by the things that we can control and those that we cannot control. It is imperative to know the things that are within your control and those that are not. In life, the things that we cannot control are too many of those that we can control. For instance, we cannot fully control what can happen to us, the people that surround us, and what they do and say. We cannot fully control the health of our bodies and our preferences, among many other things. The thing that is controlled by us is the way we think and perceive the things that we see, hear, and taste. Therefore, the secret is that you can control our happiness by changing the perception of things.

If you can distinguish or identify the things that you can control and the ones that you cannot, then it will be easier to live a stress-free life. When faced with a situation, it is, therefore, good to exercise through having a conversation with yourself, asking yourself if whatever you are dealing with is in your control or not. For instance, you are moving to a new neighborhood and because it will have neighbors who got there before you and those who will find you there. Therefore, you have no control over the king of neighbor that you should have, and this should not worry you. Just develop a positive attitude towards the neighbors that you have and the ones you might have in the future and try to cope with them. Again, you are not fully sure putting on the right attitude will surely lead to a good neighborhood because you have an idea if they will notice your effort and reciprocate. Therefore, just be happy that you have the right attitude, and the rest will just fall in place.

Journal

The day is always full of many activities, and some of the activities are repetitive in nature. You realize that if the activities are repetitive, if you do not look at the critically the way you do them, there is a likelihood that you will do the same thing over and over, probably repeating the mistakes or doing it incorrectly every day. Some people wonder why they do not grow socially, intellectually, and economically. This is because they do not have a routine of keeping daily journals of what they have done during the day.

Journaling should not only include what you have done during the day but also how you have done it. The journal should also show a list of good things that you have done, and those that you think that you have not done well could be given a description of how better you can improve to make it better. Improving yourself is striving to be a better person every day, and therefore, your daily journal on how you have improved and where you plan to improve and how you plan to do it should also be recorded.

All the record in the journal helps you in growth. The part on the good thing that you have done gives you motivation; when you do something good, it brings positive energy on your side, giving you a forward force that will enable you to do more good tomorrow and in the future. The part for what you have not done well gives an indication that you should improve; it gives information on the specific aspects that you are supposed to improve on. The reflection on what you have not done well gives brings about critical thinking that gives options on how to improve and helps to evaluate the options to find out the better option.

Having this exercise at the end of every day is important as it motivates an individual to strive to be a better person. It also shows progress as the daily evaluation helps to know what you have achieved and what you have not. It also acts as a guide to what one wants to achieve in the future.

Practice Negative Visualization

Everyone is expected to be positive about the future and not think about negative outcomes. It is called keeping positive energy. This is not the case when it comes to stoicism. Stoicism allows an individual to practice negative visualization because it is not everything that would be positive even if you have done everything right. This exercise helps an individual to imagine the things that might go wrong in the future and prepare for them in case they happen. This exercise starts by looking at the plans that you have in the future and reviewing them one by one, and rehearsing how they would be done and the required resources. The people involved in the plans should also be looked at and their availability; remember, if you are going for a long journey using a car, the driver of your car might get sick along the way, even if he has taken all the precautions and his or her body is in good condition. Also, people have their plans, and when you plan to include them in yours, their availability must be conformed and planned for, but it does not mean that they will be there for you. This does not mean that your plans stop, always have an alternative. Therefore, you should take care of the eventualities by having another driver with you.

This exercise ensures that you put everything into its place; somebody said that failing to plan is planning to fail. You should not allow failure to find you; plan for it so that if it arises, you have ways to go around it. Failure also makes people frustrated, and depending on the personality and how serious it has affected you, it can have an effect on your mental health; having control of the future and the negative happening expected makes you have control of the future.

Amor Fati (Love Everything That Happens)

Sometimes we regret or feel bad when something happens, and it is not in our favor. It is not easy to control what happens in the world; therefore, it is better to embrace the attitude that what happens is for a reason and when it happens, do not worry about how it happens; be happy, regardless of whether it has happened in your favor or not. People who practice stoicism concentrate only on what they can control, and the events of anything that they cannot control; they leave it to fate. When something that is out of control happens, it is a reality because it is already done, and therefore accepting it is the only thing one can do. Accepting it means that it should not bring unhappiness to anyone, and instead, one is supposed to love it the way it is. The essence of this attitude is that, even if you become unhappy about it, there is nothing you can do about it; you cannot turn back times to undo the action, and even if you do, still you cannot do it differently because you have no control over the situation.

Some things, which are to happen in the future, also exhibit the same characteristics. Even if you struggle with all your energy, fate will remain the same. Therefore, there is no need to strain yourself for it. For example, when you are going for an interview, and you are stuck in traffic, there is nothing you can do if that is the only route and means of transport to the interview location. Even if you walk, it will take you more hours, and you will still be late. The only thing is to accept the fact that you are going to be late and pray that whatever happens when you reach the location of the interview will be in your favor. However, if it does not work out to your favor, just accept it as good and feel happy again, because you have no control over the situation. Holding on the event makes you miserable; things happen, and they pass; therefore, it is not healthy to attach yourself to what you wanted to happen or what you like.

Chapter 9: Stoicism Is Ideal for the Real World

In the past chapters, we have already had an in-depth glimpse of stoicism and how it came to be. We have looked at the history and background of stoicism, not forgetting the Greek and Roman stoicism. This chapter focuses on the relationship that stoicism has with the real world. As we have earlier seen, stoicism refers to the non-display of feelings even when you are going through so much.

The stoics in a bid to develop practical guidance for everyday life developed three disciplines by the use of ethics, physics, and logic. Logic forms a basis when it comes to sane thinking and making a sound judgment. This basis is requisite in order to decode the next arms. We move on to physics. Physics entails the comprehension of human nature, and how the world is composed is a basic element in a bid to secure how the world works. When we have a basis for this, we are able to lead our lives in the best way possible. Which is known as ethics? The guidance was then divided into three disciplines, namely, assent, desire, and action. This was the works on one Epictetus. Although there exist these distinctions, all three of them marry each other.

Epictetus explains three things that a man ought to associate themselves with if they want to be mentally apt. What we desire and what we averse. This is in a bid to ensure that you get what you desire, and you do not get into what you averse. This involves careful living. Second, comes locomotion. This is how an individual moves about. It involves not falling into recklessness. Thus staying careful in whatever you do. The third is that of assent. Assent entails not displaying your emotions even at the worst of events.

Assent as a Discipline

The discipline known as assent corresponds with logic. The discipline has an effect of creating a distinction between the behavior of human beings of reason and animals. This is because it entails the process of sheer seeking knowledge, which often leads to acquiring it, then decoding the knowledge. According to the Stoics, human beings get knowledge from what they may have experienced in the past. Moreover, they buy from the school of thought that as social beings of nature, we have some inborn predetermined concepts that gauge our moral behavior. Before we grant or deny something, we use reason in order to make a judgment. This judgment is often a result of assenting to something or failing to do so. This has also been referred to as phrenosis. Phrenosis refers to the process by which an individual is able to employ practical wisdom in his everyday activities. This entails making the right decision whenever necessary. Today the act of using practical though can be referred to as mindfulness. Mindfulness entails making the right decision whenever necessary.

We are encountered with various events in our lives, and what is of concern is not the event rather but how we respond towards the event. Take, for instance; somebody does something wrong with you. You will be inclined to respond in any manner that you wish. Although you have to keep in mind that every response has a consequence. Your mind as a tool is what decides what goes on throughout your day. Your mind will be the reason you engage in various activities and why you respond to various stimuli the way you do. The consequences of your actions will always follow you down the road. This discipline relates to the right thoughts and the implication of reason in order to guide oneself.

The discipline of assent manifests itself in various ways in our lives. Take, for instance, you are driving down the alley, and a pick-up truck comes and hits your bumper and then drives off quickly. Your first reaction towards the incident will be to come to an emergency stop. You will then curse the driver who was in the pick-up truck as he or she drives away. When you heard the hit at the back of your vehicle, you came to an abrupt stop. This is what is referred to as the use of emotions in a correct manner. You were shaken because things were not in their status quo, and thus, you decided to stop and make sure. When you rested assured you were safe, the feeling of anger came out as depicted by the loathsome quarrels that you let out towards the pick-up truck driver. The anger comes in as a result of using emotions in the wrong way. The events have already taken place, and there is no need for you to be angry at this point.

Anger will only serve as a disadvantage to you because you will be emotional and thus easy to make mistakes. The rage can make you affect more accidents. The stoics related thinking according to nature with living according to nature. This involves the correct use of your mind in making rational decisions. The process of thinking was thus divided into two. This involved one that was according to emotions, thus intuitive thinking and another that is according to reason.

Desire as a Discipline

The discipline of desire can be linked to control. We all have an understanding of what desire is. Desire refers to the want of something. When you desire something, you are in complete want of that thing.

The idea that lies beneath the discipline of desire is easily comprehended. In life, we are defined by our social classes and our abilities in one way or another. No matter how hard we try to overshadow this fact, this is the veracity of what happens. For instance, there are things that are in our control and those that are not. Those that are in our control, we are able to manipulate them in a manner that we desire, but those that are not, we can do very little about them. For instance, there are things that are under our direct manipulation. This includes but is not limited to: reactions, desires, and judgment. There are things that are not in our control, however. We try to control these things by giving it our all. This may include our goals, the ones that we set in order to achieve. They may be long term or short term. There is often a fifty-fifty chance of succeeding, thus when engaging in something; it is of great essence to consider the odds. The odds may not always be in your favor, sometimes the situation may change, and you need to know how to respond when this happens.

Many religious topics have related to this topic by drawing reference from their various prayers. For instance, a prayer seeking God to give us the calm in accepting who we are and what we cannot change. We fall into a deep depression, usually because we want to influence changes in what we have no power over. We care much about what others think about us and not what we want for ourselves. Our friend's feelings and opinions are out of our scope of what we can influence. We have no control over that. Focusing on that will often bring you stress because you will not get the desired results.

Imagine a scenario where you are about to go for an interview. Here you need to focus on the things that are going to be a plus one to your resume. If you let your anxiety disorient you to an extent whereby you are in the worry of the interviewee, how they may react to your responses, you shift your desires to a place where you have no control over whatsoever. The feelings of the interviewees are born with them, and they will stay with them. Your manipulation is not in their jurisdiction. Your best approach can be to focus on how best you will do your part. This will play a big role in aiding you to move closer to your job. Creative thinking is a method by which you engage your mind in the sheer analysis of thoughts that will build upon your situation.

Desire needs to be tamed in order to fit in the shoes of our capability. Taming of desire requires meditation peacefully. You are in your own world, and you can visualize what you are in the reach of and what you are not. Meditation also brings you to the present and relates you to the situations at hand. You are aware of what is not in your control, and thus you can respond positively towards it. Our ability to stay present to the current situations is heightened. When we embrace the act of being present, decision making becomes easier for us.

Action as a Discipline

We all engage in various actions as a result of various triggers that manifest themselves in our lives. Right action is often rare.

People will act on impulse and regret after. Your response thus, your action has to be cultivated in a manner that suggests you have a sense of direction. An action combined with another action will often lead to greater action. In order to achieve something great, you need to do things step by step. Often you have heard someone refer to the saying of a journey of a thousand miles. Persistence and perseverance are what wins the day. When you achieve one action at a time, you will realize the magnitude of this at the end of the day.

Boldness and courage are what is embraced when performing an action. Shyness would often cause the action not to effect. The force applied in action is not a raw force. It is a skilled force directed towards your best interest. Why do we act? We do this in response to various triggers to our pressure points, forcing us to give up our stationary nature and adopt one that is locomotive. This is the definition of right action. When we are faced with obstacles in our lives, the solution often lies with the right action.

There include three facets that act as an aid when determining the right action to take. They include meeting rhythms, metrics, and priorities. With these tools, you are in a position to have a forecast about what will happen in the future. You can weigh the consequences of an action before engaging in them.

Priority helps you to weigh your problems in a hierarchy. This hierarchy enables you to weigh your problems in a manner from the one that requires an immediate response to the others that can wait. This way, you are able to solve your problems systematically. You do not dwell so much on the problems that have a lower implication in your life. Metrics will entail the analysis of the consequences. With this, you are able to anticipate the consequences. Metrics, in its sense, entails measuring the diversity of something. With metrics at hand, you are able to act accordingly and in the right manner. You will always way your options before settling for a particular option. Your actions will not be rush but rather well-thought through. Metrics will also be of advantage in your everyday life. When you weigh your options correctly, you are in a position whereby you will not find yourself in trouble all the time.

With meeting rhythms, the same way you are ready in the face of trouble, you will be waiting for opportunities to knock on your door in order to maximize on them. You will not overlook opportunities, and you tread carefully and smart. Trading smart has an effect on making an individual succeed in whatever he or she is doing. When you are faced with trouble, you will be in analysis of the various responses you can assume and be ready to take any when the need arises. Taking action is often thought through process and not by an event.

Chapter 10: Manage Your Emotions to Find Inner Peace

We encounter various instances in our lives, and how we respond normally is a reflection of how we feel. How we best to control our emotions will have an effect on how we respond positively to various situations. There are various techniques that we can use in order to manage our emotions.

Practice Deep Breathing

Science has it that when you take a deep breath, you increase the production of endorphins that will result in heightened brain activity. This way, you are able to feel less tensed and anxious. Fresh breath carries with it a fresh supply of oxygen, which is important in keeping your brain apt. Simple breathing programs have been seen to be great relievers of stress. You can make a habit of doing these exercises whenever you feel like your emotions will overwhelm you. Before engaging in a breathing exercise, there are a number of things that you need to consider. The spot for this exercise should be a comfortable place. Your mode of clothing should be one that does not cause distraction. Deep breathing will come on its own, and it is a need-not force issue. You do not force deep breathing, but rather, it comes on its own. This practice can be done twice a day. These exercises do not last for long in that they will not take much of your time.

A misconception that has always prevailed with people is that they tend to take shallow breaths as a remedy for deep breaths. Shallow breaths have the effect of shutting you down. Your energy is shut down with short, shallow breaths because they tend to increase the anxiety rather than diminish it. Imagine you are panting like a dog in the face of trouble, this may even end up with you passing out. Before you get on with the breathing process, take note that you should: Make sure you are comfortable, it can be a horizontal posture with a pillow under your neck, or it could be a seated posture on a chair with your head and shoulders supported.

When breathing, let air flow in through your nostrils, let it fill your lung cavity, your ribcage will always respond by enlarging while your air sacs will be filled with air. When breathing out, it should be through your nose too. In order to feel this movement effectively, you need to put one hand on your stomach and the other on the chest. You need to do this repeatedly in order to achieve the desired results. The process of breathing should be one that encompasses the brain too. While breathing, make sure that you are keen enough to focus. You engaged in the breathing exercise in order to feel relieved. In order to achieve this relief, you need to close your eyes and picture an image that brings out the best feelings in you. This will be often reflective, or it can take another form.

Surround yourself with peace. In order to achieve this, you need to imagine that the air around you is warm and welcoming. When you do this, you will visualize this peace from its entry point to your body until the time that it exits the body. You feel the airflow all the way. In this manner, you are also able to visualize your troubles as they leave you, and you separate yourself from it. You can consider embracing the use of a phrase in order to maximize the effects. The procedure can take an average of ten to twenty minutes in maximum. The lengths of the breaths should be increased as you advance in your routine. This achieves more results.

When breathing, makes sure that your muscles also participate. Practice a routine whereby as you take in air, you contract your muscles in a bid to feel tensed. Release this grip as you exhale. Your muscles should relax in synchrony, flowing the systematic arrangement from the feet all the way to the head. Each muscle should be tensed at a time in order to achieve maximum results. This way, the muscles participate, too, and you are able to achieve maximum relaxation. Your last breath should be the one that pushes all your troubles away.

Find Your Inner Power

When we are in the face of trouble, linking ourselves to our inner strength will see to it that we rise from the trouble, and we are able to move forward. There are a number of ways that will see to it that you connect to your inner self and that you are able to rise. The various success stories that have come from numerous people who were able to connect themselves with their inner power. For instance, below are some exercises that will see to it that your inner strength is elicited and that you are able to use it in a manner that is advantageous to you.

Believe in yourself

When we do not believe in ourselves, we are insecure about the occurrence of a particular set of facts. This is because we have not accepted in ourselves that we can be accepted because of our various strengths. Various strengths will manifest themselves with side effects as weaknesses. When we are insecure, our inner strength is diminished greatly. In order to achieve believing in yourself, you need to practice accepting who you are. When you have feelings of like towards yourself, you are able to like the world around you more.

Practice Silence

We live in a world that you may not know what is going on in somebody's life. Due to these distinctions, the world is filled with confusion every now and then. This can be a distraction to you when you are focusing on achieving your own self goals. Taking some time to stay in silence plays a big role in making you refreshed. Furthermore, you are isolated from people, and you can think on your feet. Silence means that you are devoid of anything that elicits noise. This means no technology should be involved. When you achieve silence, your inner chaos is calmed, and you are able to connect with the strength that exists inside you.

Repetitive Program

We often do things in a shoddy manner because our inner energy has been drained. When an ounce of our physical energy is used up, our inner strength is also used up. The effect is direct. You want to find your inner self, and the best way you can do this is through separating the activities you engage in daily into separate simple and achievable portions that you can achieve progressively throughout the day. When you do this, you are in a position to do these tasks in a repetitive manner, and with this, you can achieve mastery. When you achieve mastery, your brain is at ease. When your brain is at ease, you have created a lot of space in it.

Check on your circle

We respond in discrepancy, especially when we are around various people. The same way that different people have a way of making us feel in some type of way. When you are around a bad company, your inner energy will always be diminished when you meet them. They fill you with information that has a tolling effect on your inner energy. They often dwell on filling you with their inadequacies, which in turn will make you feel sucked off the juice in life. Look for people who have a positive impact on your life. People who will make you bring out the best in you. Optimism is what you look for when you are seeking a circle. There are people who feed you with positive energy. This type of energy is important in building the inner you. Most of the time, after a conversation with these guys, you will find that you have cultivated a culture of thinking positively, which boosts your inner strength.

Impression

Research has it that what you feel inside will often find its way to the surface. The vice versa also works as what is perceived in the outside is a representation of what is on the inside. Exercising and feeding properly will see to it that you remain proper in the outside. Your dressing should be also in a manner that makes you feel best about yourself. When you are concerned about your health, you are in a position to make sure that your body is in good condition. Ti refers to both internally and externally. The body comprises numerous parts, some of which need keen consideration in order to know when they are in jeopardy. When you create a good example on the outside, you are in a position to influence your inner self the same way. This way, you boost your confidence.

Link with Your Energy Source

The spiritual sphere has been seen to be the most effective when I come to connect to your inner self. This is not limited to one religious sphere, but rather it is diverse. Meditation will link you to your inner energy when done in repetition. Meditation is key because, during this time, you visualize yourself as being alone. In order to effectively exhibit your inner strength, you need to create a link with the spheres that surround you. The sphere around you is greater than you, and this is what puts it in a position whereby it can multiply your inner strength. When your inner strength is multiplied, it has an effect on your physical strength too. You believe that you are in a position whereby you can achieve more even though your physical energy does not say the same story.

Focusing on Self-Love

On the basis of love is the feeling of self -love. This is because you cannot claim to extend the feelings of love to another person until you extend them to yourself. Self-love is at the peak of healthy living. This is because it will be a determinant of the many factors that will stick with you all the way. Self-love does not merely entail the feeling of good. This is more than that. This is being in a position to appreciate yourself from a deeper context. Self-love manifests itself in the doings that make our lives worth living. When we appreciate our lives, we are in a position to appreciate ourselves, and it is only then that we will start to appreciate others. Actions that make us grow are what make self-love possible. The diversity of self-love extends to how well we accept our inadequacies. How we adapt and live with them all our lives appreciating the fact that we are human. The acceptance of human nature is one that entails a keen understanding that we have shortcomings just as we have strengths. In order to achieve self-love, there are some pointers that an individual may use. They include:

Mindfulness

Mindfulness is directly attached to self-love because people who practice mindfulness are in a position to take note of how they feel, what they want, and what they are thinking. They are careful enough not to trade on the grounds that will have an effect on them. Mindful people will think through an event before deciding to take part. They will analyze a situation in terms of consequences even before they decide to engage.

Priority

Priority is key when practicing self-love. With priority, you are assured of satisfying your urgent needs before you proceed o wants and not vice versa. This concept may seem remote, yet it carries a higher concept. There are people who participate in impulse buying; these types of people will always acquire what they see when they like it without an inner contemplation. With priority, you will be able to analyze the situations at hand in terms of wants and needs and as a result, find the perfect criteria in which you can acquire goods.

Self-Care

Self-care is at the bedrock of self-love. When you care about yourself, the effect is often that you will extend some degree of care towards yourself. Often people who have been found not to extend some degree of care towards themselves have been said to have no love towards themselves. This is because care and love go hand in hand.

Boundaries

Creating boundaries goes a long way in trying to exhibit self-love. When you create boundaries, you are in a position not to be affected by the emotions of other people. When we get carried away in the emotions of others, you will get angry at yourself all the time. You will be concerned about the feelings of others rather than yourself. This way, you do not love yourself.

Gratitude to oneself

Gratitude entails being thankful for all that facilitates your well-being. Gratitude can be directed to oneself or to other people.

Gratitude has some aspects of mindfulness in that it will entail the recognition of the deed before gratitude can ensue. A reflection on the topic of gratitude will often make people think of materialistic gratitude. People view gratitude as a great thing and often forget that it can go as basic. When you are kind to other people, that is a simple way of expressing your gratitude. No matter how remote this act may seem, it often has implications that are deep-rooted. What sits in between a totally awesome day and a bad day is the distinguishing acts of gratitude.

Self-gratitude happens in a bid to appreciate oneself; it could be through the situations that you have had in life. Self-gratitude happens as a result of a monologue with oneself, telling yourself that you have so much to be thankful about. Self-gratitude is also buried deep under the concepts of self-care and self-love. Practicing gratitude is as easy as it may be and is also as effective as possible when done in the right manner. A single word of gratitude said to someone will often go a long way. You give gratitude to yourself because you are in a better position of noticing your life advance than others. Most of the time, you may expect to receive gratitude from others, and when this is not the case, we tear down in emotional disgust. Being grateful to oneself boosts the overall confidence of an individual. When the confidence of an individual is boosted, the individual is in a better position to achieve more in life.

Self-gratitude can be a daily routine, something that you do to remind yourself how great you are. In order to achieve self-gratitude, you need to have a gratitude statement, one that you repeat daily. In order to achieve more, you need to set achievable goals, which are short term and work on achieving them step by step. Make sure that you take note of inspirational quotes that are effective in building your self-esteem at the onset of the day and throughout the day. Approach a reflective outlook whereby you focus on how far you have come. Looking back at your past experiences play an important role in helping you to move forward from your previous experiences.

Forgive Easily

To some people, according to forgiveness to someone is easy, whereas to others, it takes more than the words. Egotistic people will often feel like they do not wish to exhibit forgiveness, whether it is asking for it or offering it. In order to adopt a culture of forgiveness, there are a number of things that you need to take note of: When you are wronged, you will first experience anger, which will seek to take control of your body. Anger makes us decide on a no basis manner. This is often because we feel that we have the ever-rising need to respond. When we are wrong, we ought to take some time and let the anger flow past you before you can be able to respond. Normally the response to anger is spontaneous and may often result in a consequence that you did not desire.

In order to effectively forgive someone, you need not rush the process as forgiveness is a gradual adventure that ought to take steps before you can effectively say that you have forgiven someone. When granting forgiveness, one ought not to feel obligated, but rather, this needs to be a good feeling one that elicits good vibes. Before forgiveness, one needs to practice acceptance that the set of facts are the way they are and will not change. We need to change to adopt overriding circumstances. Acceptance is processed by which you are directing your thoughts towards finding a remedy to what has already taken place. Forgiving can be life-changing if you set your mind to it, and you do it.

People often draw feelings from their past. From these feelings, they carry experiences that made them feel that way in the past. An individual will feel bad when the same kind of story keeps on repeating itself in his or her life. Imagine the same grievance happening to you all over. This I possibly an indication that you did not forgive and move on. Forgiveness entails distancing yourself from the narrowest of thoughts that arouse past experiences that may make you not forgive. Though forgiveness may take some deep reframing, it is worth it in order to effect recovery.

With forgiveness, you focus on the events taking place at the moment, and you stay devoid of the past. Feelings of the occurrence might be depressing. This is what makes you even reconsider forgiveness. Allow the stress to leave you. When you achieve this, you are in a position to let go through forgiving. Breathing deeply can help a great deal when wanting to control the effects of something. This will calm your body and mind leaving you devoid of stress. When you are devoid of stress, you are able to make a sound judgment. Forgiveness is a gradual process. The moment we understand this is when we will easily achieve it.

Chapter 11: Ways to Manage Anger Using Stoicism

Because of the emphasis of Stoicism on understanding your emotions, anger comes on top as an emotion that we could use to manage how we feel.

In the book *The Meditations*, philosopher Marcus Aurelius detailed on how we could use Stoicism to help us manage our anger better. In the book, he outlined ten different strategies with which we could manage our anger. They were gifts, he said from the Greek God of healing, Apollo, and his nine muses.

Remember That You Are Not Perfect Either

Stoics considered it paramount that to adhere to the therapy of the philosophy, one needed to come to terms with their flaws.

Seneca noted that anger affected even the gentlest of people and that, therefore, to effectively work on managing your passion, you needed to admit it to yourself. In the world today, cases of people going to extreme because of the rages of anger have been well documented, with examples of domestic violence, crimes of passion, and homicide lending credence to this fact. Therefore, you would want to lay your anger on someone means that you, therefore, are not in tune with who you are.

The view by Seneca, therefore, means that to use Stoicism would require that you take a pause and think of how you would potentially do things to people that would get them angry. It called that while you pointed your finger at another person, the other three were led back at you, and therefore, you were at risk to be at fault just as much as the other person was.

So this call for us to admit that we were just as likely to commit the offense done to us would then make us take a step back and view the situation more calmly and rationally.

Aristotle believed that anger was not all bad and was justified in some instances. Therefore, when you acknowledged this, you would be able to realize then that another person's anger, therefore, would be justified. Therefore, by admitting to yourself that you are not a perfect being would mean that you would also become more willing to extend empathy to the other person, as you will know that, had you been in their shoes, as offended as they are, you most likely would have reacted the same, or similarly.

Thus, when you become more in-tune with your faults as a human being, then chances are high that you will prioritize the need to view the other person through non-judgmental lenses. When someone steps on your shoes, you then admit to yourself that it is a mistake that you also would have made.

However, this admitting of wrong does not mean that becomes willing to let people get away with being incorrigible assholes. Indeed, it would make you better at assessing people and bringing you more in touch with the essence of humanity and, thus, become more able to see others through better lenses.

It's Not the Behavior That Upsets You, and It's Your Opinion About It

One of the most important questions that you can ask yourself is that -is it that specific behavior makes you angry, or is it the person?

One of the ways we show cognitive dissonance when it comes to emotional responses, and most importantly anger, is that depending on the context, we tend to allow or let go of a particular behavior even when we admit to ourselves that we do not tolerate the behavior.

Look at it this way. You visit the park; a place is teeming with people. You join the others in making the best of your time there. Then, a confrontation between one of the employees of the parks and a visitor ensues. It's a shouting match and threatens to come to blow. You look at the two as people unable to control their anger. You learn of what led to the blow-up and are not impressed. So, you point at a castigating finger at them. But, supposing it was a friend, would you castigate them too? Chances are, you would possibly defend them, feeling their anger was justified because you understand the context.

When put in context, the reason why we get angry could be down to how much emphasis we place on particular behavior and traits. For this reason, then, you will find that some things will make you angry but not make another person upset, or it could make another person angry but not you.

Therefore, to become better at managing your anger, knowing what makes you angry, and why is important. This would allow you to understand the context and how it influences your reaction. You will also be able to understand better why another person got angry about something that did not raise more than a curious glance from you.

Understanding how our opinions shape our emotional reaction to things is vital in developing ways in which we can become more rational and better at managing our anger. This would also allow us to come to terms with the cognitive dissonance that makes us castigate certain people when they are angry for justifiable reasons and defending others.

For stoics, this view on what drives your anger on certain things would mean that you will be able to reconcile yourself with whether you are placing too much emphasis on things that re beyond your control. Placing too much emphasis on things that you cannot control will most often result in heartbreak for you. Always. And this could make you angry even more. This could take a toll on your emotional state. As Seneca stated, we need to confront our anger as an enemy - away from the center of our emotional chambers. Allowing yourself to get angry at situations that are indifferent to your well-being would mean that you would then not make any productive progress with your anger.

Your Anger Does More Harm to you Than What You Are Angry About

How does it feel when you are angry? It's so - draining, right? There you are, apoplectic and exploding like volcanoes. Your heart is racing violently, sending tearing sensations through your chest like it's about to burro itself out of your sternum. Your body trembles and you are barely breathing fine. Your head thuds and your thoughts grind to a halt. All you see, then, is what made you angry. This is certainly not the best feeling.

Now, of course, there are medical repercussions to getting angry, which include, but not limited to, HBP.

According to Stoics, anger makes you ugly. It distorts your features and makes you an unpleasant grotesques creature that is cringy to look at, and we don't want that. But of course, being unpleasant to look at is not the end of it. This is just as a start, and perhaps you are already ugly, so this effect doesn't affect you much. Well, there is a reason this point doesn't end here.

Consider this scenario. You buy a new phone which you have been saving for months. You are ecstatic and jubilant. Wow! Its features are just astounding. You float away to your friends. You want to show off your new phone. And you get there, and they are all happy for you. It goes on well until one of your friends, as they attempt to take a selfie, drops it to the ground. The screen shatters, and with it shatters too your dream of spending some quality time with your new phone. You are livid! You accuse your friend of jealousy and stomp out.

Your anger clouds your mind, and you do not take note that you are ruining the friendship. According to Stoics, other people's actions that make us angry only harm our outside - our possessions, maybe our bodies - but when we are angry, we harm our very core. Anger clouds our better judgment, which would make us react in a manner than injures our character. By limiting our ability to reason, anger could be the reason why you lose friendships and relationships. It could be what costs you your jobs.

When you understand that what you are angry about is something that you could deal with and still maintain your character, you become able to then deal with it productively.

Before letting anger take control of you, begin by thinking about what it will cost you and whether that is more important than what is making you angry at that moment. Chances are, what is making you angry is not worth your character. It is not worth indulging in the draws of anger if it will result in you losing people you love and value. It is not worth indulging if it will cost you your job.

Marcus Aurelius went as far as to state that one needed not to be angry at people that they consider kin, as this went against the Stoic Principle of Nature that said that we should work together. This means then that you should never let your anger overtake your love for the people close to you. Speaking broadly, we can also interpret this view as not to be angry with our fellow human beings.

They May Not Understand Why It's Wrong

Socrates once stated that no human being did evil in their knowledge. As such, when someone wrongs us, the natural impulse is for us to seek then ways in which we can take revenge on them.

In the broader view of this, people will often defend what they are doing when they are questioned about it. Concerning the countless events that have happened in the world in the past, when we look at them, the perpetrators of these heinous acts felt that they were doing the right thing. They weren't harming other human beings, you see, they were defending their people. In their twisted way, they felt that they were doing the right thing. This view is controversial and seems to justify why the people committed it. But this view is to instead bring to the surface how we will defend what we do in our heads.

Seneca summarized this view when he gave an example of how one would not kick a donkey back or how one would not bite back a dog because the man felt that they did not know what they were doing. As such, he called for us to extend this to our fellow human beings then. Rather than respond to anger with anger, he called for us to rid ourselves of it and then make a point of trying to rid of the other person of it too.

Our need to condemn and vilify people that offend us could be counterproductive in that we may find ourselves exhibiting the same blind spot when in a different situation where we are the angry one.

Once more, understanding that someone doing wrong could not be aware of how wrong it is not to justify the fact that they are wrong. Instead, it is to bring ourselves much closer to how we act and react when confronted by a situation or right and wrong that we may not be aware of.

As such, rather than repay wrong with our anger, this calls for us to make an effort to make the person more knowledgeable on why their actions were illegal and why they will need to change. This view is what is shaping the current movement in many countries to make prisons reformative rather than punitive. To punish one who did not know why their actions were wrong would only make them more likely to do the wrong deed again. They would have anger, which would make what they do feel justifiable, thus, creating a vicious cycle of anger birthing anger.

Even in Anger, Be Compassionate

The above point segues directly into this one.

When someone wrongs you, it only becomes natural that you will then see it fit that you punish them. In trying to punish them later, you put yourself in a situation where you become angry too, and again, in punishing them, you make them mad and spiraling from this, generations of anger.

Aurelius stated that when someone made him angry, what he would do is first dealing with the feelings of anger within. As we have learned in this chapter, this would involve understanding your imperfections and how your opinion shapes your rage. Once he had done this, Aurelius would then take the person aside and explain to then calmly, about how in their moment of anger, they were doing themselves harm and not him. This belief that an angry person deserves help or to be educated helped him then become more cool-headed into his later years.

Seneca called on us to not judge other people based on failings that all of us are bound to fall short of from time to time. He called for tolerance, making the point that, if many people had pardoned their enemies, was it not right then, to forgive someone that makes you angry by little actions?

Through calling for us to become more tolerant and patient with other people's behavior, Seneca and Aurelius then made it known that they wanted us to think through our anger before acting. Thus, it was easier to give the other person the benefit of the doubt when you took the time to process your passion before reacting to it.

A belief that, unfortunately, several people hold seems to be that showing compassion is a sign of weakness. More affected by this are many men, whose trait has been termed as toxic masculinity, which encompasses a lack of empathy, a glorification on unproductive anger among other negative characters as inherently male.

Seneca called on us to put our trust in someone that showed an understanding towards a fool. He called on us to reject the first incentive of rage, which often calls us to seek to punish the other person. Through the building of compassion, which is an inherent human emotion, we will be able to become better at managing our anger. When we make it a point to take our time to understand why someone made us angry, we then become better at putting our thought before our actions when we are mad. This helps us then become better at conflict management through de-escalation.

In Book Two of *The Meditations*, Marcus Aurelius, stated that in life, you would come across people who bore unpleasant traits, ungrateful and violent, unsociable. But such people, he said, seemed not to have the knowledge of what was good and what was bad. Instead, as a person who has taken the time to understand the implications of your actions, and especially under the intense passions of anger, you would then take the responsibility of persuading the other person on why their actions of anger were injuring them more than the people that they intended to hurt.

When you become more compassionate, you then begin to see how, indeed, in life, very few things need to get you angry. This would make you live a more fulfilling life and become better at how you treat people and how you manage tense situations.

Chapter 12: Understanding How and Why Anger Rises

That we will get angry is not something that we can debate about nor disagree with. As with other emotions within us, it will come from time to time, with varied triggers and of course, calling on us to react to it in a variety of ways. In a bid to manage our anger better, we need to understand how and why.

Understanding the Reasons Why

We get angry for very many reasons. A friend that can't stop meddling in our affairs can send us up the wall. A person that you don't like can get a rise out of you just by existing. Someone unable to take in simple instructions can raise your hackles. Therefore, learning of our triggers was key to helping us control our anger.

The reasons are as vast and different as the number of people that exist on the planet. Whether anger was justified or not is something that still has philosophers in this modern-day cross swords. Aristotle believed that anger was justified in some instances. Aristotle said that getting angry at the right time and with the right reason made anger right. But while this was true, it became hard to determine how to measure what was the right time and what counted for the right reason. As we have said above, and in chapter 11, the fact that our beliefs and our opinions about things made us then determine what made us angry makes it difficult to find common ground then.

Seneca was categorical in his belief that anger was just a vice with no redeeming quality. He viewed that passion made us slaves and that once one allowed themselves to be overtaken by the emotion, then they would not slow down.

Looking at this, it then becomes critical to us that, in a bid to make ourselves more rational and in control of our anger, understanding what makes us angry and why is essential.

This knowledge would then allow us to break through the situation where we get angered by inconsequential events or opinions. It becomes paramount then that we know the reasons for us being angry are productive and, thus, that we should then allow ourselves to feel this anger.

Getting angry at your friend for breaking your phone would be counterproductive since it would mean that you would lose a friend if you expressed your anger, on top of the fact that the consequence was external and, thus, easy to confront and conquer. However, getting angry at an injustice lends credibility to Aristotle's belief that there was a period when, indeed, we are justified to get worked up.

However, even with the understanding of good and evil, we needed to be aware of the fact that the other person could be doing the wrong from the point of ignorance, thus, approaching them with a desire to educate them rather than punish.

With is in mind, it becomes easier to know if you need to get angry or not. For the most part, anger is damaging to you, and it is best to avoid getting tangled in its tentacles.

Distancing From the Appearance

When you have seen how destructive anger is, you will begin to decide then to work on it.

Stoics then call on us to take our focus away from the physical and into the spiritual.

Seneca stated that our goal should be to attain a tranquil mind. This state, he said, made it possible for the Stoic to then remain calm in the face of a tempest of rage and fury.

Appearances can be deceiving, and thus, will mislead us into thinking that a situation requires our attention when it doesn't. Take note of when something is offered to you with seeming the express intention to make you angry. Anger, according to Seneca, is a binary emotion, taking charge of you as soon as you are well aware of it.

This then means that you would be easily swayed under its sweeping wings when you were obsessed with what was in front of you. We have seen this many times. An example of this being a scenario called 'outrage porn,' where someone, or at times the media, shares a story whose main intention is to create a rise out of people. Through cheap sentimentality and melodrama, they use this focus that we have on the efficient processing of data, meaning that we will get angry at what is directly in front of us. When you make the attainment of mental tranquility your focus then, appearances begin to matter less. When a story is shared with the express intent of making people angry, instead, you go further into the story to find out if there is any justifiable reason to get angry.

By emphasizing what is merely in front of you, you become less reactive and more in control of how you interpret things. You understand that there is more to what you are seeing. When someone is angry at you, you do not get mad at them in return, because you know that there could be more to their anger than just you. You'd also know that the violence is doing them more harm than good. You will take personal lessons from the teaching of Socrates that tell us not to do wrong or repay evil with evil, no matter how right it feels or how justifies we think we are.

Emphasizing appearances then will mean that you become more aware of how to put your express your frustrations to the other person rather than just snapping. You will come to understand what it means when you have to choose your anger. Does expressing your frustration lead to productivity? Or does it harm? After this, you then make a better distinction between whether it was the circumstance that made the other person angry or if they were indeed mad themselves? This then determines how you would proceed.

Reminding Ourselves of Our Humanity

In an incident that happened later in his life, Aurelius was presiding over a court hearing that involved a volatile billionaire Herodes. In a moment of the exemplification of the consuming madness of rage, Herodes lunged at Aurelius but was stopped by a guard, who wanted to impale Herodes with his sword. But, Aurelius stopped him and adjourned the hearing. Throughout the incident, Aurelius remained calm and collected, not betraying any anger. As a lifelong student of Stoicism, Marcus Aurelius was able to maintain and indeed acknowledge the humanity of someone who seemed hell-bent on harming him.

This is one of the more significant teachings in his books, The Meditations. When we become angry, we tend to look at the other person out of the context of their humanity. Through distortion, we reduce the entire other person's existence into this one instance and, thus, see them then as objects that deserve to be punished because of failing us.

But it is this kind of problematic thinking that led to Seneca declaring that anger was a danger to humanity as it could easily be infected from one person to another. This behavior is typified through 'mob psychology.' To make people come together and work as one cohesive until often takes resources and management, yet, it seemed to be that anger got people cooperating quicker. This was because led on by the desire for destruction, people quickly reached into their basal instincts and acted upon that as since it is easier to let yourself get carried away by your primal urges, it is easier than for anger to let us devalue another person and thus, act in a manner contrary to what we collectively share as human beings, our collective conscious.

Seneca called on us to heal rather than punish those that wrong us. Aurelius asks us to look at ourselves in the eyes of the person that angers us, or that hurts us.

Through seeking to correct the other person rather than punish them, we will then act in a manner that views and acknowledges their humanity and, therefore, the truth that they are prone to make errors and that the incident with you is but one of the mistakes.

Look back at when you were angry at someone. Did they seem to stop mattering? What mattered to you in that state of anger was that they had wronged you, and they needed to pay. This then meant that you overlooked the reality that they may have abused you because they didn't know better, or that the people were also dealing with issues of their own that they did not know how to handle it. We come across such people throughout our lives. People that do wrong without the knowledge that they are doing wrong.

Pausing to understand that they could be ignorant of what is widely considered right or wrong could go a long way to making you deal with how they act towards you. Again, this doesn't mean that you excuse bad behavior. Instead, you become more aware of how other people's actions shouldn't affect how you react.

Removing Ourselves from The Competition

Social comparison, as psychologists call it, is a form of state of being where measure our progress by looking at how others in a similar situation are doing.

This comparison is advantageous to us for a variety of reasons. For one, by looking at where others are, we understand better where we are and where we are going. It also offers us a peek into what qualities we would want from the other person and incorporate that into our own. This is what has driven us to build the things we have.

Through social comparison, then, we get competitiveness. In a bid to be better than the other, we become driven by the desire to stay ahead consistently. However, competitiveness has a side effect – anger.

Imagine the number of times that sportspeople have come to blows when the tensions run high. Imagine the anger that seethes in you when your friend, who supports another team, goads you when their favorite team wins more trophies and beats your favorite team.

When taken to the extreme, called compulsive competition, this anger at competition may result in a person becoming livid even when there is no apparent reason to be. Because of the nature of competitiveness, everything becomes a competition, meaning that anger is always lurking.

To manage your anger, take yourself out of the competition and instead aim for a more tranquil mind. Aurelius calls on us to eschew things beyond our control that make us angry. These things include competition. You will never be ahead of everyone, and this realization is what we should then use to guide us in working on our anger.

In one of his most important teaching, Aurelius called on us to work together, following the Stoic principle that saw us all as kins, and thus, we worked better through cooperation rather than through conflict, which results from competition taken to its extreme.

Putting this to practice is something that, indeed, can and will be challenging. Throughout our lives, we have known competition as the way to exist. But you should turn your mind to the law of abundance, which states that there is enough for all of us. Rather than view another human being as a threat, we view them as another team player, eager to build humanity like the rest of us. Making ourselves our competition then means that we will guide our actions based on what we can control, rather than putting faith in outward forces that we cannot control and whose happening is widely erratic and unjust.

Fulfilling Our Roles towards Others

This view that we are here to exist in harmony is a significant part of Stoicism. Throughout his book, Aurelius spoke of our obligation towards our fellow human beings, suggesting that 'we were born for something other than this' about our anger at our fellow human beings.

Socrates called on us to fight the urge to repay evil with evil and wrong with wrong. There was nothing right in doing wrong.

When we look at the text of Stoicism, we begin to understand that, through calling on people that adhere to it to get more in touch with who they are, the philosophy is calling on us to become better human beings by understanding our failings and our strengths.

The four virtues of Stoicism all call for us to fulfill what will, in turn, be of value to the other person. Through an insistence that we focus more on events that we can control and not on external factors and circumstances, we will be able to understand ourselves better and what we stand for.

It is indeed unfortunate that many of us claim to be standing for justice or truth or morality but then turn out not to be espousing the virtues to their core. This is not based on the nature of humanity to error. When someone claims to be moral and asks others to be virtuous, but then act consistently in a manner that is not in contradiction with what they claim, then it is not a case of human error but rather, a failure by the person to properly understand what the value entails.

We see this all the time. Someone claims one thing in public, but then it turns out that they are doing the exact opposite in private. When caught out in the double lives, the claim is always that this was an error. But to espouse the virtues of Stoicism, one needs to be well aware of who they are and if indeed they do value their thoughts concerning other human beings. To become selfless, you will need to understand the depths of your selfishness. To then become a just, moral, and person of courage, you need to understand how you have perpetuated injustice. You will have to come to terms with your moral failings.

When you can be more forgiving to yourself of your failing, then you will also extend this forgiveness to others when they fail. You become better at teaching what you value.

When you don't espouse these values, but make a claim to uphold them, what will happen then is that to prove how deeply you value them, you will be punitive to people that err genuinely in their journey to become better. You do this to calm your guilt about not upholding these values. You do this to make those that esteem these virtues applaud you, which is why the loudest moralists turn out to be scam bags. The purists turn out to be nothing more than loudmouths. The people that claim to be may turn out not to understand how justice functions.

Thus, as an obligation to the people around you, and humanity in general, become more in touch with your person. Understand who you are, your emotions and feelings, your beliefs, and actions. Know then, that you can do better and make the effort of doing better. To fulfill your role better to others, then, means to fulfill your role better to your being.

Chapter 13: Stoic Philosophy and Anger

Stoicism calls for us to examine ourselves and use that to make the world around us a better place.

Thus, anger was one of the main issues that Stoics faced and attempted to dissuade us from falling into, as it is the beginning of the fall from a virtuous existence. It's not hard to see why? Almost every one of the stoics virtues, courage, wisdom, morality, and moderation, fall apart when you get angry.

Because of this, the Stoic Philosophy has a few lessons for us concerning anger.

Anger is Madness

At least temporarily, at least. Seneca calls on us to avoid it, as, even when it is justified to be angry, acting out of anger still never results in a positive outcome. He stated that, while every other emotion affects our judgment, passion went on and disrupted out the state of mind. It made as insane for the duration of the anger. A look at social media sites will indeed offer you a glimpse into the madness that is anger. People write and print all things that they would otherwise have not done had they taken a moment or two to deal with the exploding feelings.

So, to become angry was to go mad. To manage this, then needed to take a pause and question our anger. Chances are, it was unnecessary.

Anger Makes Things Worse

Marcus Aurelius stated that the effects of rage were bound to be more than the circumstances that led to it. When you get worked up at your friend for breaking your phone, that would only worsen the friendship and cost you your friend. Getting mad at another person will only result in a broken relationship between the two of you. Getting angry at an inanimate object will work you up for nothing.

In all these instances, anger works against you in every way at the end. Your character suffers, as you then become someone that people will want to avoid. When you argue with another person, it then means that they have a reason not wish to associate with you. Anger lingers on long after you have presumably expressed it. It is what led to Seneca to see it as something that, once gets a hold of someone, it became difficult to wrest back control.

To Deal With Anger, We Need to Acknowledge Humanity

The view by Socrates that no person ever does out to commit wrong willingly ruffles a few feathers, but it is crucial in helping us deal with anger.

Through the lived experience, Stoicism encourages us to take a moment when angry to see how the other person may have a life beyond the state in which they exist in that particular time – the state of 'this person made me angry.' When you look at the person as a whole rather than the parts, you then become able to understand their actions and, thus, why you should not allow yourself to become angry.

Thus, you then shift your focus from seeking to punish this other person, an action that would make you angry, towards telling them how their works of anger are harming them. You become more compassionate.

Chapter 14: Stoicism Reveals Rituals That Will Make You Confident

Probably, you have read hundreds of articles either online or elsewhere, about how to make yourself happy, become confident with yourself by exorcising negativity from your life, and boost your self-esteem so that you can live happily with yourself and everyone else around you. Yet, you are still stack in negativity, and you have not become a thousand times happier. So, you find yourself confused and begin to curse yourself for investing your time reading stuff that doesn't work. You are not alone!

There is a fundamental difference between reading stuff and putting what you have learned into practice. You don't expect to read good books on cooking and then become the best chef in the world! You must put that knowledge into practice, and invest hours of experimenting with it so that at the end of the day, you emerge victorious as a result of the knowledge you gained from the books. You will never kick like Bruce Lee by merely reading martial arts books. You must go out there to train and practice your behavior, to make the necessary changes and adjustments.

That is why the stoics, the ancient masters of wisdom, didn't write stuff for mere reading. They went a step further and created rituals and exercises that had to be performed daily to train the mind to respond positively to life events so that one can live well and happily. They warn us of the danger of getting satisfied with the mere reading, without practice and training, because with time, we forget what we had learned and begin to do things the other way.

Today it is fascinating to see modern scientists agreeing with what these ancient masters of wisdom used to talk about many centuries ago. We can't help then but to turn our mental eye back and look into what these gentlemen suggested may years before we were born.

Things happen in everyday life that make us feel like we are not good enough. When we make a mistake, or when something unpleasant happens to us, we find our brain making a replay of every other failure and mistake we have ever made. Just like that, our self-confidence gets crushed, and our self-esteem dips. This is an old problem, and as long as there have been people in the world, they have gone through such experiences. It is an ancient problem with ancient solutions. Ancient stoicism comes to our aid during such times. They realized that unless we learn and practice to question irrational thought and unhealthy beliefs that crush our happiness, we cannot perceive ourselves or the world clearly for a better, fulfilling life.

They understood that our feelings emanate from our thoughts. But the question is, "How do we get rid of our irrational and unhelpful thought that crush us, and allow rational and helpful thought to reign in our minds." Here is how we can use stoicism rituals to achieve that.

Identifying and Challenge Distorted Thoughts

This ritual is about learning how to monitor the voice in our head. That voice in our head passes harsh judgment to us when we are down. Let's say that you have engaged in a particular project, and then it fails. The initial thoughts that come with such experience are usually irrational and unhelpful. The voice in your head begins to condemn you for having wasted your resources, making futile attempts and makes you think that you are a complete failure. Due to such thoughts, you begin to feel down, unconfident, and uncomfortable with your abilities.

The Stoics knew that identifying such thoughts was an important step. When your self-esteem dips or when you are gripped by a feeling of lacking confidence in yourself, what is the voice in your head telling you? This is a way of getting beyond the feeling and looking into what is causing such a feeling. The aim is to identify the thought system, which is behind it. So you need to be able to follow your thinking process and capture the thoughts which are pinning you down by generating feelings of worthlessness.

For example, "I felt sad because I thought I was a failure." Or "I felt unworthy because I thought I was used up and taken for granted." Identifying such thoughts is vital so that you can move to the next step of challenging them. Capture thought like:

- I'm a complete failure
- I'm stupid and foolish
- I'm an idiot
- I will never amount to anything
- I will never get a job
- I'm ugly and disproportional in shape

These are initial thoughts which come in your mind when life events crush you down. The stoics suggest you identify such condemning and distorted thoughts and challenge them. But how do you test them? After identifying these thoughts, here is how you can challenge them: for every distorted thinking, provide a rational thought to replace it. Look at several examples below:

- **Distorted:** "I have invested a lot of my time and effort, but finally, I have not achieved anything. This project has been a sham, and I wish that I had not started it!

    Rational: "Even though I have not achieved what I had intended, I have learned a lot through my mistakes. I will learn from my mistakes so that I will not repeat them in the future. I'm a young man with a lot of potentials."

- **Distorted:** "I will never get a job. I lack the courage to stand before the interviewers, and any time I do, I shake uncontrollably. I'm doomed to fail."

    Rational: "I will have to do something to master my confidence during interviews. I will practice in front of the mirror and practice public speaking in small social meetings before my next interview."

- **Distorted:** "I'm not beautiful. My shape looks awful in the mirror. Any time I get into a relationship, I get dumped within two months. I'm awful, and nobody loves me."

    Rational: "I need to take control of my weight and get back to shape. I have ignored my weight loss program for two years now. I'm great and beautiful, but I have to make some little adjustments."

Test Your "Core Beliefs"

This is about the beliefs you have about yourself. Sometimes, these chronic feelings of lacking confidence and having a poor image of oneself go beyond negative thoughts. Lack of faith in oneself can be a direct result of having negative "core beliefs." There might be an inner critic inside you who presents consistent evidence to you about the kind of a loser or unlovable person you are. As a result, you come to believe that lie because you have not taken your time to challenge such belief by questions its validity. The stoics prescribe that we should make it our habit or ritual, to challenge or core beliefs.

Challenging your beliefs is not easy, given that such a fundamental idea may have already taken roots and are now forming the basis of every decision you make. Confronting that layer who wants to prove his case that you are a loser by always presenting concrete evidence in your head can be a daunting task.

The first thing that you need to do to deal with this lawyer who keeps on prosecuting you and condemning you to be a loser is to analyze the kind of evidence presented on your end. Write a list of proof as to why you feel that you are unworthy. It may sound funny, but this step is essential. The stoics suggest that you write down everything that makes you believe that you are a loser. You need to analyze and understand the evidence of this prosecution lawyer so that you can devise the best method to poke holes on it.

What you have been lacking is a defense lawyer on your side, to address the negativity confirmation bias that you have suffered. With your inner voice aggressively presenting evidence to you as a loser, you end up seeing things in your life that agree with the idea that you cannot amount to anything.

To counter that, the stoics argue that you should also make another list of evidence. This list acts as evidence that the lawyer prosecuting you from within is wrong. It should have all the reasons and ideas that prove that you are not a loser. This new list of evidence aims at altering the settings of your beliefs so that you stop noticing the unhealthy feelings and force you to look at all the things that have happened in your life to see the evidence that supports your healthy beliefs.

The stoics also suggests that you find a co-counsel. You need a friend or a family member or any other person you can trust, to remind you of what you are excellent in, by pointing out all the great things that you do. Getting such confirmation from someone you believe makes you feel valuable and important, and bring to the surface some crucial evidence that you may dismiss by seeing it be insignificant. Even if they see things like counting, that you don't think should count, put them on the list. This list of concrete reasons as to why you are valuable and impressive will help you to silence the prosecutor from within by replacing the biased evidence of negativity with the evidence that is rational, accurate, and honest.

Have an "Evening Confidence Ritual"

After digging deep and addressing your core beliefs, your inner critic will still attempt to linger on. The change will not come overnight. You need to keep on programming your mind so that you can fix all those false beliefs and prevent them from popping up again. The Stoics understood thoroughly the power of an evening confidence ritual in fixing negativity and keeping it at bay. They knew that by taking some time to reflect every day can bring tremendous improvement. It is an excellent way to watch over yourself by taking sometime in the evening to review your life.

After confronting your inner critic with all the reasons as to why you are not a loser but a winner, the battle continues. Reflect on your life by taking some time at night and think of all the things you are good in and what you have achieved that day, and come up with more evidence as to why you are not awful. Since now, you have become less reactive on yourself, accumulate a daily evidence log to enable you to develop healthier beliefs.

Reviews are essential, and they are common in business, especially annual reviews. The stoics knew the power of reviewing one's day to improve the quality of life. Sometimes you need to look back into your past to understand your future. Think of what you have done during the day and ask yourself whether it worked well for you. Reflection makes it possible for you to monitor your daily life by thinking of how the activities you have engaged yourself in have helped you to become better. Do not hide anything from yourself, or pass anything.

Reflect on what you did right and the thing you didn't get right that day. Reflect on the things that you were supposed to do, but you dint do them. Such knowledge is vital as you plan on how to improve your tomorrow. Don't condemn yourself for the things you didn't do or the one you didn't wrong. Learn from your mistakes and forgive yourself. Having self-compassion and forgiving yourself is what prevents you from repeating mistakes as well as avoiding further procrastination.

Don't beat yourself up or be critical of your abilities. Capitalize on the thing you did well during the day, and use them as a basis for doing better tomorrow. Appreciate yourself for the good things of that day, and continue doing them tomorrow. It is a great way to extend your blessings. Promise yourself that you will not repeat the mistakes of today tomorrow, without being critical or judgmental. This is a master key to self- improvement, and happiness. As time goes by, your positive belief will become prevalent, and the inner critic will begin to go silent.

Use a "Cognitive Cue Card"

At this point, you have identified and challenged your thoughts, dug deep, and scraped your negative beliefs, and you are making an awesome follow up by taking an evening review of your daily life. But there is one more step if you are to realize stoic self-confidence. You need a cognitive cue card to help you monitor further the negative chatter so that you don't give in to it. A cue card acts as a quick reminder, and it contains frequently used information, such as reminders and prompts.

Sometimes when you are distressed, you need a quick response to wipe out such distress within a moment's notice. You need a way of challenging that inner critic any time no matter where you are. You need a way to make such a challenge smoother, instead of spending a lot of time arguing with yourself. This will help you avoid the back and forth that can make you look like an insane person.

There are those negative thoughts you are accustomed to, and you keep hearing them so often. That is where a cognitive cue card comes to your aid. You need to have a set of immediate responses to such thoughts so that you can counter them with positivity immediately they appear. Write such responses on your cognitive cue card so that you will not have any difficulty remembering them.

Sometimes you are tired of arguing with yourself. At such times you may notice that your mind is heading in the wrong direction. That is the best time for your cognitive cue card to come to your aid. Use it to counter the obvious negative thoughts and keep your interpretations rational.

In the heat of the moment, a three by five notecard comes to your aid in enabling you to keep doing better. It helps you to think differently during less-calm moments. So, during tranquil and less calm moments, writer down on your cognitive cue card the things you believe you would want to hear during stormy times when you are tired with less time to argue.

For example, when you face failure, you can have a cognitive cue on your card, which says, "Just because I have not achieved my goal, it doesn't mean that I'm a loser. By learning from my mistakes, I can achieve greatness." Carry your card with you and use it to learn to be self-compassionate. It is not going to be easy, but by repeatedly practicing to tell yourself sensible and rational stuff during awkward moments, you will finally master this stoic ritual.

Programming your mind with stoicism rituals will take time. Sometimes you will screw up, but consider that to be normal. Continue reprogramming yourself by taking small steps of practice every day until you realize your wellbeing. Don't be a perfectionist as no one feels 100% confident, but focus on progress as you continue to become better. You have a right to be confident.

Chapter 15: Stoic Philosophy Ancient Wisdom in the Modern World

Stoic philosophy is a different school of thought from other schools because it teaches practical wisdom. Its philosophy is anchored on actions. The belief of stoics is that application is the end, while debate and thought are just a means to that end. The stoics teaching of self-control, virtue, and tolerance has been a great source of inspiration to both thinkers and leaders for many centuries. They believe in four cardinal virtues which lead to happiness and fulfillment in life. These are courage, wisdom, temperament, and justice. Now the question is, we should practice these virtues in our modern world to live with confidence, fulfillment, and happiness.

Striving for improvement

Stoics believe that change is constant. A lot of change is happening in the world today, more than any other time in history. Yesterday's solutions may fail to work for today's problems. But these stoic principles are eternal. They work all the time. They can help us learn to change with the times and keep learning new things as the world changes. New knowledge will help us to see opportunities instead of whining about the challenges.

Face the world as it is

To face life with confidence, we should learn to meet the world as it is. Stoics believe that we should learn to appreciate the world as it is, instead of debating for years on how it should be. There is nothing wrong trying to think outside the box and bring changes, but that can only be done after we have first appreciated our world and accepted our place in it.

Don't worry about what is beyond your control

You are at the airport. The management announces that the next flight has been canceled because the weather is not conducive. You begin to yell at every airline worker you come across. What good will that do to you? You will only wear yourself down with unnecessary stress. Who is responsible for that? You have no control f over the weather. Stoics teach us to only worry about what is within our control and direct all our resources towards it. Worrying over what we can't control doesn't solve anything. This is important if we are to live happily in our modern world.

Keep a journal

In our modern world, we need self-reflection more than ever. We should learn to document our lives so that we can monitor our achievement by recording our ideas, plans, and goals. Taking time to reflect on our progress, achievements, success, and failures will help us have better ideas on how to live happily in our modern world, which is changing very fast. Stoics knew that, and that is why they advise us to reflect on our daily activities each time before going to sleep.

Chapter 16: The Four Cardinal Virtues

Cardinal virtues are the essential moral qualities that a person needs in order to lead an upright life. A person with cardinal virtues acts right in all aspects of their life because they have high self-control. The virtues are also in line with the scripture.

Wisdom

It is also called prudence virtue. It is said to be the mother or source of all the other virtues that follow. This is the first virtue because, as the name suggests, it deals with human understanding and intelligence. This virtue involves a person understanding the right things to do and actually doing them. By the use of this virtue, all human beings have the ability to tell what the right thing to do is and the wrong thing not to do. When someone chooses wrong over right, they are just ignoring the wisdom virtue. However, this does not mean condemnation for people who do wrong, as sometimes the mistakes are genuine. It, therefore, calls for seeking other's opinions and advises before making decisions on things you are unsure of. Some people are very good at telling them right from wrong, and those are the people that should be sort for help. When you ignore your prudence and others, you are merely imprudent. One cannot practice the other virtues when they lack prudence because they have no wisdom to determine and follow through. Wisdom will show someone the effects of doing something and the consequences of not following through things.

Justice

This is the second cardinal virtue, and it comes second because it is all about a person's will power. The willpower to do what is right to ourselves and also to others. To give another person what is rightfully theirs, we need to have the willpower to do that. Otherwise, one may be aware of how to do right but does not do it because they lack the willpower to exercise justice. When doing the right things to others or exercising justice on others, nothing should stop us. It does not matter how much we dislike the person or how much below our class they are, what is rightfully theirs should be accorded to them. If someone became your enemy after they had given you money, as a person exercising justice, you should pay them back. This is because the enmity has nothing to do with the justice you are, according to them. Justice is positively giving someone what they deserve, no matter how helpless the other person is. When someone is denied justice, it is called an injustice. The person has been denied what they deserve even when they have a legal right to it. Even when someone is not bound by the law to do what is right, the conscious will tell someone what is right. For this reason, even those who feel above the law should practice justice. This is because the natural instincts of justice are within each one of us.

Courage

This is also known as fortitude and is the third cardinal virtue. This virtue deals with the courage to conquer any sort of fear and be firm in our willpower. When we get rid of the fear, we are able to face any difficulties in life. However, having courage doesn't mean that a person should go looking for trouble to prove they are courageous. It merely means that when the danger comes after us, we have the willpower to face it instead of running away. Therefore, the virtues of wisdom and justice give us the ability to tell right and wrong and how to exercise them. Courage gives us the strength and willpower to implement the two other virtues. Without courage, one has wisdom and knows what is right to do, but they lack the guts to actualize it. This is a gift of the Holy Spirit as Christians believe. Not everyone is gifted with courage. Courage will make a mighty man give respect to a very common man because they have the courage that helps them realize that it won't make them any weaker doing what is right.

Temperance

It is also called self-control or moderation virtue. It strengthens courage virtue. This is because courage helps do anything without fear. However, without self-control, one may end up doing the wrong things thinking as a showoff of courage. It helps a person put aside their own personal desires when there is a greater reason to help others. If a person does not have temperance, they do not care about others, they will only do what is right for them, and it is usually selfish. Temperance gives us the ability to balance things out. Yes, our needs are essential, but if having these needs will be harmful to others, temperance restrains us. It is also through temperance that we are able to deny ourselves of 'too much' on things because too much may be harmful. Temperance sets the limits for us; without this virtue, there are no boundaries on things that we do. It helps a person say stop when they have had enough of something, and it is time to stop. For example, food is good and an essential means for our survival, but when we overeat (binge eating), it becomes harmful. If someone were to have anything they wanted without self-control, there would be a lot of destruction. There would be a lot of immorality in society if people ignored the virtue of temperance. It also means that people can use drugs; however, they want because they do not control themselves. Without self-control, people would steal and kill as they please. It is therefore very important than no matter how powerful a person is, they practice temperance.

The four are, however, are not the only virtues, but all the others that come after are somehow connected to the four. However, without even adding other virtues, the practice of these helps people co-exist with respect and peace. It is essential that everyone learned to practice these virtues because, from this, all other virtues will be easy to follow.

Chapter 17: Incorporation of Stoic Philosophy into Everyday Life

Stoicism is the ability to let go of things and situations that are not in our control. Most times, we want things to go as we plan them to, and when they don't, we get frustrated. Stoicism helps us let go of this burden of letting go of things we cannot control. Stoicism gives hope at our most desperate times, right before we sink into depression for worrying about things beyond us. As human beings, we are always trying to make things our way, and this gives us anxiety for overthinking things. The best remedy for fighting this is practicing stoicism no matter how difficult and depressing the situation is. Ignoring stoicism will only cause someone pain because, in the end, if it is beyond you, there is nothing you can do about it.

How to Practice Stoicism

The most important thing is to realize the things and situations that you can control and know what is not. When you know what is beyond you, it helps you not to waste too much energy on something beyond you. Knowing that something is beyond prepares you for any results and therefore enables you to avoid unnecessary stress. You help your mind realize that the outcome might not be favorable, and therefore you are able to deal with any issue. When you do not establish what is beyond you, your mind goes through a lot of stress because it feels like one is merely weak. Each person needs to know that everyone has something beyond them, no matter how strong, powerful, or wealthy they are. Changing our perspectives on things we cannot control protects us from damages that would result from constantly worrying.

We should learn to work on improving ourselves. Knowing what our limits are is good, but it does not mean we relax or lose hope. Some things are beyond us, but there is always something we can improve on what we cannot control. Learning to grow in different areas is a stoic principle because it encourages us to keep practicing instead of giving up. However, improvement does not mean perfecting. We cannot perfect something beyond us, but we can improve on that thing if we do not give up but instead keep practicing.

An example of this would be given in a classroom set up. A student may be very poor in mathematics, and they have done the best they can, including private classes for the same. Stoicism dictates, instead of focusing on it and being depressed because it can lead to failure in the other subjects, the student should work on improvement. This does not mean that they work to be the best in math class, just that they should not quit trying, especially in a compulsory class. The practice may take them from a poor percentage to a better one that counts a lot.

We should also strive to live our lives exactly the way life happens for us. This means finding something to be grateful for in every situation. Sometimes life will be unfair, but instead of stressing about this, we should take every opportunity to learn from it. Accepting that we cannot always get what we want gives us inner peace. Stoicism also means that we accept people in our lives and try to co-exist. You cannot change people; we all have different feelings, thinking, and ideas. We should be able to accept each other exactly as they are. Trying to change people will only hurt you as a person. A person can only be changed by themselves. However, if we change our attitudes towards how we react towards people, we do not agree with, this is stoicism.

Taking action instead of giving up is a stoicism practice. Stoicism means you let go of things beyond you, but it does not mean you sit back and relax. It does not mean that you quit taking risks and start feeling sorry for yourself. Things don't just fall into place; we work hard to get things to happen. You cannot control the situation, but you can manage your actions by using different strategies. Maybe things are not working out because you always do them in the same way over and over again. Change the strategy; you might not get the exact result you hoped for, but you will achieve an outcome, good or bad. It is an outcome that should be a lesson for you. Accepting you have no control is not enough, you have to go and try to get things done but in line with the moral values. You do not want to try to compete with something beyond you and end up in trouble. So this means that whatever you are seeking is in line with the cardinal values so that you are protected.

Practicing stoicism also means that we discern right and wrong and making sure to do what is right. This means practicing the four cardinal virtues, which are prudence, justice, courage, and temperance. When you practice doing what is correct, it means you are able to give value to everything around you. People want to be rich; no one ever wants to be poor. Stoicism comes in that you live right. You do not have to steal from people so that you become rich. A stoic person will work hard and let riches come to them naturally. However, someone who does not practice stoicism will take the action of stealing, corruption, and all the bad virtues to acquire wealth. How you react towards any given situation determines how much stoicism you practice. A stoic person always tries to follow the virtues and let things flow as they should, but the opposite person takes power in their hands and tries to do all the controlling.

Take prevention measures for anything that could go wrong. You cannot control your body from ever falling sick, but there are some diseases that you can prevent yourself from. Take preventive vaccines for those diseases. This is called the prevention of misfortunes. Prevention of misfortunes means always having your mind prepared for any disaster that may befall you. Being ready helps a person be in control of their emotions in events they cannot control. It means that you are prepared to surrender to the events but very in control of happiness. Being ready for misfortunes means that any bad results will not determine your joy because you have already accepted the consequences beforehand. When you are mentally prepared that anything can happen, you then make plans for a plan B or even C. It means you have not placed all your eggs in one basket because you well know they could all break. Being ready for misfortune does not mean we are anticipating for bad things to happen. It only means we are ignoring the likelihood of things going wrong. The reason people are so overwhelmed by circumstances in life is that they are caught by surprise. Not being in control of circumstances does not mean we cannot protect ourselves from any harm that may befall us.

Stoicism also encourages that you keep a record of all your day's happenings. A journal is essential because it acts as a reminder of things we are likely to forget. We make decisions in our minds to do something or change something. However, it is very easy to forget things only if we think about them. Writing about things we intend to work on, we help us keep check of ourselves. A journal also helps someone look at their progress from where they started to where they are right now. A journal enables you to get the pattern of how you do things. You could be thinking something is beyond you because you keep failing. Then using the journal, you realize that you have been using the same strategy all the time. A journal will, therefore, help you note places you can work change on. You can change your plans very fast even before the end results because of a pattern an alert you on time. When on the road to improve on something, the journal gives us a routine. When you have established what to practice on, you need to keep working on it. A routine will help you not change your plans along the way before you have achieved your intended goal. We cannot fully trust ourselves to remember everything; each moment we learn something new, we always end up forgetting the old stuff. If something was recorded, however, it will be unforgettable because you can still read it through. A journal also helps us appreciate ourselves better. Instead of being too hard on ourselves, we can look at the journals and see things we achieved. Some things we achieved were once too difficult for us, but if we met those, then we are reminded we can achieve anything. Journaling, therefore, encourages someone to take risks they would never have considered.

But most importantly, journaling helps us know ourselves better. Not only does it help us realize where we fail, it helps us understand the strategies that work for us, and it also helps us see the very many obstacles we have overcome.

Chapter 18: Growing Up Stoic (Philosophical Education for Character, Persistence, and Grit)

Parents and guardians are encouraged to teach children about philosophy at home. This means teaching children how to handle any obstacles they are likely to face in life, as early as possible. For the parents to do this, they have to be aware of the real virtues which they are expected to pass to their children. Stoicism says that virtues are inborn; we are born with the ability to tell right from wrong. It is, however, up to the parents and guardians to ensure that kids do the right things. Our happiness and personal satisfaction are gotten when we do the right things in life and being of good character. When children are made to practice virtues, they eventually become good and can control themselves from making random mistakes and poor decisions in life.

It is not enough, though, for parents to teach their children and be strict with the children to do right. Parents and guardians must also practice what they preach. This means that they have to be a perfect example of what they teach. When a child is told to do something, they are more likely to do it if they watch their parents do it. This is not to put pressure on the parents to be perfect; it merely means being real with your child. Let your child know that you are also wrong sometimes, but you always strive to be right. Let them learn how to move past the several mistakes that they make in life by being an example. Teaching the child can be derived from the following virtues.

Justice

This means teaching your child to be just and fair in all their doings. Therefore, a child should be taught to be kind to others. When they are kind, they will feel for others when others are in pain and need help. When a child is just, it means that they are able to put their interests aside to help others. Children who are not taught this are very selfish and do not care about the pain they implicate on other kids. A child who is just trying to protect others who are not being treated fairly and that they do their best to be fair on others. The child is even willing to go out of their way to make others happy by helping when needed. Only a child who has been taught justice can do all this.

He Goes On to Say

In this, a parent is encouraged to create ways of making the child more charitable and able to say no to things. Some kids usually get everything they have and do not realize that other needy children do not even have the basics. Teach your child that that thing they are crying for is not as important as they think, and they can do without it. Teach your child to forego luxuries and help the more disadvantaged kids. This can only be encouraged by exposing kids to situations they have never experienced. Let them go and see the homeless kids and see how they survive. The chances are that the child will say no luxury the next time and ask that the money be used to help the homeless children they saw. In short, this means letting a child have a say in kind gestures because they already know that there are more deserving people out there. The child should be encouraged to help out more than asking for things they may not need.

Determination

Virtue encourages parents to help their children get determination, which is basically giving a child the courage to do things. This can be achieved by allowing the kids to help out in chores at home when they are still young. By helping out, children are getting life skills like courage, determination, and confidence to do various things. When they are helping out, they learn about hard work and why determination is essential to keep pushing on. They get the fulfillment after they are done helping out, which is the result of the determination.

Moderation

This virtue involves teaching children how to be moderate in doing things. Controlling their emotions, controlling their eating, and managing everything literally before it becomes too much and harmful for them. Just like adults, children also have felt they need to know how to handle. It is, therefore, important to sit your child down and talk to them about their tantrums. Let them know that it is alright for them to be angry, but it is also essential that they control it. Teaching a child to be moderate in their decisions involves letting them assess their situations. Ask them if they think their tantrums were worth it, and if they believe there is a better way, they would have communicated their frustrations. This will help a child see for themselves how they would have been moderate in their emotions. In eating, kids do not understand why they have to eat certain foods. They want to eat only sweet things. They should be taught why moderation is good at eating. Why it is essential for them to eat healthily and why it is essential not to overeat of whatever they want to eat.

Wisdom

This virtue helps a child know right and wrong, have the proper judgment on things, and accept the things beyond their control. A parent can help the child by sitting with their child every day in the evening and together analyzing the child's day. Let the child say the things they think they did right and the things they feel they did wrong. Help the child know what they would have done differently so that the next time they are in a similar situation, they can make better decisions. Encourage the child if they are feeling helpless for things they had no control over. In doing this, you are instilling wisdom in your child. A child will be able to make better decisions in the future and even be able to let go of things beyond their control.

Conclusion

Stoicism is very important in society; it can be attributed to being the reason why the world is peaceful. It is due to stoicism that people are able to co-exist. Stoicism is very fundamental for every single person whenever we are facing hard times. During hard times, stoicism gives us the hope to wake up, dust ourselves off, and press on. We are taught to let go off of the things we're unable to control. Without stoicism, we would all sink into depression because we all go through hard times. Nations would fight each other because there is no control, and a country can go after another as they please. But because we have stoicism, we have globalization. Nations with different people of different cultures and colors care and help each other. That is why nations will send relief food to nations that are going through war or drought. Stoicism is also the reason why nations will accept refugees into their countries.

It is through stoicism we learn that our failures do not define us. Therefore, instead of worrying that we failed, we try different strategies. We learn through stoicism that we all have weaknesses but that we have the ability to move past our shortcomings if we practice stoicism. We learn to be real with ourselves, to forgive ourselves for things we did wrong.

Our leaders are able to deliver for the people only if they practice stoicism. This means that they put the people's interests before their own. The reason why we have increased corruption, injustice at the courts, and increased immorality is because leaders do not practice stoicism. As rational human beings, we are able to live peacefully with our neighbors despite them being too different from us. We accept them with all their flaws and look past them because we understand that we cannot change them. It is also through stoicism that we are able to keep ourselves from judging people when they do things we do not agree with. Letting them do whatever they want as long as it is not hurting us.

It is through stoicism that there are courts of laws. This is to help people who feel they are being treated unjustly to get the justice they deserve. The lawbreakers are also imprisoned to help correct them because society wishes the best for them. Without punishing the criminals, then the courts are not being fair to the victims.

Stoicism helps us appreciate life. We stop looking at situations and feeling sorry for ourselves when things are not working out. Through stoicism, we are able to appreciate the little we have and the ability we have as individuals. Being grateful for everything, no matter how life makes us love life and look forward to brighter days. As humans, we learn to have empathy for others, and we also get the wisdom to help us in life. Stoicism is, therefore, very important and should be practiced by every person in society. We can only be able to understand each other as human beings if we are all willing and determined to practice stoicism.

Finally, if you found this book useful in any way, an honest review is always appreciated!

www.ingramcontent.com/pod-product-compliance
Lightning Source LLC
Chambersburg PA
CBHW072009070526
44583CB00015B/1401